SASQUATCH UNLEASHED

THE TRUTH BEHIND THE LEGEND

BRIAN KING-SHARP

CONTENTS

INTRODUCTION

Welcome to a journey that will take you deep into the heart of one of the most enduring mysteries of our time. This book is not just another collection of anecdotal tales and blurry photographs. Instead, it is a rigorous exploration of the Sasquatch phenomenon, grounded in scientific methodology, personal field research, and a critical examination of the cultural influences that shape our understanding of this elusive creature.

As a Sasquatch researcher, I have spent my fair share of time in the field, observing, and collecting evidence. My personal anecdotes and experiences, which I share throughout this book, provide a unique perspective on the subject. They offer a glimpse into the challenges and rewards of Sasquatch research, and they underscore the importance of maintaining a scientific approach in the face of uncertainty and skepticism.

The scientific method is the backbone of this book. It is the tool that allows us to sift through the noise and confusion, to separate fact from fiction, and to approach the Sasquatch mystery with an open mind and a critical eye. But as we will see, even the most rigorous scientific inquiry can be undermined by cognitive biases. Confirmation bias and cognitive dissonance, in particular, can distort our perceptions and lead us astray. These pitfalls are not unique to Sasquatch research, but they are especially relevant in a field that is so fraught with controversy and conflicting evidence.

Sasquatch is not just a subject of scientific inquiry; it is also a pop culture phenomenon. From movies and TV shows to advertisements and merchandise, Sasquatch has permeated our collective consciousness. This cultural saturation can both help and hinder serious Sasquatch research. On one hand, it raises awareness and sparks interest in the subject. On the other hand, it can trivialize the research and perpetuate misconceptions. This book delves into this complex relationship between Sasquatch and pop culture, examining how it shapes our perceptions and influences the direction of research.

We cannot ignore the role of hoaxers in the Sasquatch community. These individuals, who fabricate evidence and perpetrate fraud, do a great disservice to serious researchers. They muddy the waters, sow doubt, and undermine the credibility of the field. This book takes a hard look at the impact of hoaxes and the damage they cause.

This book is intended for Sasquatch believers and skeptics from all backgrounds and all ages. Whether you are a seasoned researcher, a curious skeptic, or a fascinated observer, this book is for you.

In essence, this book is a comprehensive guide to the world of Sasquatch research. It is a tool for understanding, a roadmap for inquiry, and a beacon for those who seek the truth. I hope it will provide you with a fresh perspective, a deeper understanding, and a renewed sense of curiosity about the enigma that is Sasquatch.

I bring to this endeavor a unique perspective shaped by my diverse background. With sixteen years of law enforcement under my belt, I have honed my skills in conducting investigations and sifting through evidence to find the truth. This experience has instilled in me a deep respect for the power of evidence and the importance of rigorous, methodical inquiry. It has also taught me to be skeptical, to question assumptions, and to remain open-minded in the face of uncertainty.

In addition to my law enforcement career, I have spent several years as a podcaster and interviewer, conducting hundreds of interviews with individuals who claim to have seen a Sasquatch. This experience has given me a unique insight into the human side of the Sasquatch phenomenon. It has allowed me to hear firsthand the stories of those who have encountered this elusive creature, to understand their experiences, and to appreciate the profound impact these encounters can have.

My background in law enforcement and my experience as a podcaster and interviewer have shaped my approach to Sasquatch research. They have taught me to be both a skeptic and a listener, to question the evidence but also to respect the experiences of those who claim to have seen a Sasquatch. They have given me a unique perspective on the Sasquatch phenomenon and a deep understanding of the complexities and challenges involved in Sasquatch research.

This book is the culmination of my experiences and insights. It is also a testament to the power of storytelling, to the importance of listening to those who have had encounters with Sasquatch, and to the value of approaching this subject with an open mind and a critical eye.

Writing about personal experiences can be a challenging task for any author. It requires a level of introspection and vulnerability that can be both emotionally taxing and intellectually demanding. It involves revisiting past events, analyzing them, and presenting them in a way that is both engaging and meaningful to the reader. It also requires a delicate balance between subjectivity and objectivity, between the personal and the universal.

Transitioning from this personal narrative to a more scientific approach can be equally challenging. The scientific method demands a level of rigor, precision, and detachment that can feel at odds with the more subjective, experiential nature of personal storytelling. It requires the author to step back from their personal experiences and approach the subject matter from a more objective, analytical perspective.

In the case of Sasquatch research, this transition can be particularly difficult. The subject matter is inherently controversial and filled with uncertainty. It is a field that is often dismissed or ridiculed, and yet it is also a field that is deeply fascinating and rich with potential for discovery. Balancing these competing demands – the need for rigorous scientific inquiry, the desire to share personal experiences, and the challenge of navigating a controversial and often misunderstood field – is no easy task.

As you read this book, you will notice a shift in tone and approach. The early chapters focus on my personal experiences and field research. They provide a glimpse into my journey as a Sasquatch researcher, the challenges I have faced, and the insights I have gained. They are, in essence, a personal narrative – a story of discovery, curiosity, and perseverance.

As the book progresses, however, the focus shifts to a more historical and scientific exploration of Sasquatch research. These chapters delve into the history of Sasquatch sightings, the evidence for and against the existence of Sasquatch, and the various theories that have been proposed to explain this phenomenon. They represent a more rigorous, analytical approach to the subject matter, grounded in scientific methodology and critical thinking.

This shift in tone and approach is intentional. It reflects the dual nature of Sasquatch research – a field that is both deeply personal and profoundly scientific. It is my hope that this approach will provide a comprehensive, balanced, and engaging exploration of the Sasquatch phenomenon. I invite you to join me on this journey, to share in my experiences, to engage with the evidence, and to explore the fascinating world of Sasquatch research.

So, I invite you, dear reader, to join me on this odyssey. Let's explore the fascinating world of the Sasquatch together. Let's delve into the mysteries, sift through the evidence, and seek the truth. Let's embark on this journey and see where it takes us. Welcome to Sasquatch Unleashed: The Truth Behind the Legend.

ACKNOWLEDGMENTS

First and foremost, I would like to express my deepest gratitude to my partner in crime, Daniel. Without his unwavering support, relentless encouragement, and shared passion for life, this book would have remained a mere dream. Daniel, your belief in me and my work has been the driving force behind this endeavor, and for that, I am eternally grateful. But most importantly, thank you for never giving up on me. Even in my darkest moments, you have been my beacon of hope. Your unwavering faith in me has been a constant source of strength and motivation. You have always been there to pick me up when I fall, to guide me when I lose my way, and to cheer me on when I succeed. Your love and support have been my rock, my anchor, and my guiding light.

Your insights, your criticisms, and your praises have all been instrumental in shaping this work into what it is today. You've challenged me to think deeper, to write clearer, and to never settle for mediocrity. You've pushed me to explore new perspectives and to always strive for authenticity in my storytelling.

To my friends and family, your constant support and encouragement have been invaluable throughout this journey. Your faith in my abilities and your understanding of my passion for Sasquatch research have been a source of strength and motivation. I am truly blessed to have such a supportive network around me.

Mom. I want to express my deepest thanks to you, for being the most incredible mother anyone could ever ask for. You have always been my biggest cheerleader, standing by my side through every high and low. Your unwavering faith in me has been a constant source of strength and motivation. You have always believed in me, even when I found it hard to believe in myself. Your encouragement has been the driving force behind every achievement, every success, and every milestone I have reached.

I am particularly grateful for the way you have always supported my creative side. You have nurtured my dreams, encouraged my ideas, and celebrated my accomplishments. You have taught me to embrace my uniqueness and to express myself freely. Your belief in my creativity has given me the courage to explore, experiment, and create without fear of failure. Thank you, Mom, for being my biggest cheerleader, and my most ardent supporter. I am who I am today because of you. I am forever grateful for your love, your guidance, and your unwavering belief in me.

A special thanks to my good friend, Cliff Barackman. Cliff, your support, knowledge, and friendship have been instrumental in the creation of this book. Your willingness to share everything you have learned and take the time to write the foreword for this book is greatly appreciated. Your contributions and friendship have undoubtedly enriched this work.

I would like to extend a special thanks to my dear friend, Leila. Leila, your experience and expertise have been invaluable in the editing process of this book. Your keen eye, attention to detail, and constructive feedback have greatly improved the quality of this work. I am truly grateful for your time, effort, and dedication in helping me complete the first round of edits on this book.

To Doug, Alex, Blaine, and the rest of the amazing team at Hangar 1 Publishing, I extend my heartfelt gratitude. Your belief in this project, your professional guidance, and unwavering support have made this book a reality. Your commitment to bringing this work to life has been nothing short of inspiring. Thank you for your tireless efforts and for being such an integral part of this journey.

To Will, your keen eye for detail has helped me to refine my writing and to eliminate any inconsistencies. Your ability to spot even the smallest of errors is truly remarkable and has been a great asset in this journey.

Michelle, your understanding of the book's structure has been invaluable. Your suggestions have added depth to my characters and made the storyline more compelling. Your passion for literature is infectious and has inspired me to push my boundaries as a writer.

Wayne, your knack for understanding the reader's perspective has been a guiding light throughout this process. Your feedback has helped me to create a narrative that is engaging and relatable. Your ability to empathize with the reader has made this book more accessible and enjoyable.

And Tiffany, your enthusiasm and encouragement have been a constant source of motivation. Your positive energy and belief in my abilities have kept me going during the tough times. Your unwavering support has been a pillar of strength for me.

I am deeply grateful to all of you for your contributions. Your dedication and commitment have not only made this book possible, but they have also made it a work that I am truly proud of. I am fortunate to have you all by my side in this literary journey. Thank you once again for being the best beta readers a writer could ask for.

To all the readers who will pick up this book, thank you. Your interest in this subject and your willingness to explore the unknown are what make this work worthwhile. I hope that this book will provide you with new insights, provoke thought, and fuel your own passion for Sasquatch research.

I would also like to extend my heartfelt thanks to the amazing community of people I have met through my interest in Sasquatch research. Your stories, insights, and shared passion have not only informed this book but have also enriched my life in countless ways.

In particular, I want to acknowledge the incredible individuals and friends I have met through my role as the host of the Sasquatch Odyssey podcast. Your enthusiasm, curiosity, and shared love for this fascinating subject have been a constant source of inspiration. Your contributions to the field of Sasquatch research are immeasurable, and I am honored to be a part of this community.

Lastly, I would like to express my gratitude to the elusive Sasquatch themselves. Your existence, whether acknowledged or not, has sparked a sense of wonder and curiosity that has led to this book. Your mystery has inspired countless hours of research, discussion, and exploration. Thank you for being the catalyst for this incredible journey.

This book is a labor of love, born out of a deep fascination and respect for the unknown. To everyone who has been a part of this journey, thank you from the bottom of my heart. Your support, encouragement, and shared passion have made this all possible.

I am deeply grateful to each and every one of you who has been a part of this journey. This book is not just a product of my work, but a testament to the collective passion, knowledge, and support of an incredible community. Thank you all.

FOREWORD

CLIFF BARACKMAN

From my earliest memories, I have always loved Bigfoot. At that time Bigfoot was just a monster to me, like Godzilla, Dracula, or King Kong. Monsters were a great interest to me for most of my youth, and they continue to be to this day.

Much later in life, the realization that Sasquatches were likely real animals, and not just cool monsters, came from reading about the evidence in a small number of books, such as *The Scientist Looks at the Sasquatch*, which is a compilation of scholarly articles from *Northwest Anthropological Research Notes*. The evidence convinced me before I ever spoke with a witness or found evidence.

Brian started his path to Bigfoot in a similar way. Sasquatch was a monstrous interest to him as a boy having heard stories of several strange experiences while growing up in the mountains of Georgia. Stories are excellent motivators, but they pale in comparison to a personal experience, which Brian had when he was 12 years old. This terrifying encounter changed his life. Once the hook is set, it can't be unset.

Brian was a career law enforcement officer in Atlanta, GA. I have always found that cops are some of the best witnesses, and often excellent researchers. Their training often includes ways to be a better observer. They tend to have a deep appreciation for evidence and the collection thereof. They understand the weight of eyewitness testimony, but also its fallibility. They understand that sometimes it takes a long time to come to the truth.

An interesting aspect that Brian writes about in this book likely comes directly from his experience as a professional law enforcement officer. He makes great efforts to explain the psychological components to this mystery. Not only does he discuss possible motivations for hoaxing, but also for believing in weird things without evidential reason for doing so. He examines possible mental issues that drive people to do weird things, such as plant fake footprints or dress up in monkey suits for hoaxed footage clips.

This book is an overview of the subject through the eyes of a man who comes at the subject from several angles. He has had personal experiences. He has gathered evidence. He has spoken to witnesses. He has dealt with hoaxers. He continues to push forward to gain a deeper understanding of the subject and the animals. I appreciate his tenacity and commitment to look not only at the positive evidence in favor of Sasquatches being real animals, but also the dark underbelly of what drives the charlatans and distractors. I think this is, once again, the cop in him. Police and sheriffs have to deal with not only evidence and critical thinking, but also unsavory characters on an almost-daily basis. The truth is a destination that is always worth the journey.

1

THE ODYSSEY BEGINS

Growing up in the north Georgia mountains, I was surrounded by a world that was both beautiful and mysterious. The dense forests, the towering peaks, and the clear, rushing rivers were my playground, my sanctuary, and my teacher. But they were also the backdrop for stories that were passed down from generation to generation, stories that were as much a part of the landscape as the trees and the rocks. These were stories of encounters with creatures that were not supposed to exist, creatures that were part of the folklore and mythology of the region. The most famous of these creatures was Sasquatch or Bigfoot, as it is known in some parts of the world.

I was fascinated by these stories from a very young age. I remember sitting around the campfire with my family on the weekends, listening to my dad's friends tell tales of encounters with Sasquatch while out hunting. I went on many fishing trips with him and his good friend Elijah who was of Cherokee descent. After a few beers, Elijah would often speak of the *Tsul'kalu* or slant-eyed giant. I was captivated by these stories, and they sparked a fascination with Sasquatch and other cryptids that would only grow as I got older.

One of the stories that stuck with me the most was the tale of two ginseng hunters who had a terrifying encounter with a Sasquatch.

Residing in Summerville, Georgia, Mr. Brown is now 77 years old and doesn't venture into the woods as he once did. However, back in August 1986, he found himself in Jenkins Gap near Summerville, Georgia hunting for ginseng. He used to sell it for additional income for his family, despite being a carpenter by profession. That particular day was somewhat unusual from the beginning. He typically had a companion with him, but on this occasion, his friend was unable to join him. As he stepped out of his truck near the fire tower, he had an eerie feeling of being observed and suspected it might be a game warden on the lookout for poachers.

He made his way into the forest and began his search, descending a small hill to a flat area abundant with ginseng. While he was engrossed in digging up roots, he was once again overwhelmed by the sensation of being watched. He turned around, expecting to see his hunting companion, but instead, he was met with the sight of the most peculiar creature he had ever encountered.

A towering, hairy humanoid figure, partially covered in dried caked mud, stood before him. The creature, approximately eight feet tall, was covered in four to six-inch brown or black hair. At a distance of just eighteen to twenty feet, Mr. Brown had a clear view of it. He described it as having a large head -- seemingly resting on robust shoulders without a neck -- a medium build, and long arms that reached its knees. The creature emitted a powerful, foul odor reminiscent of a decaying animal. As he stood frozen in place, he noticed the creature's left arm appeared lifeless, with its fingernails grown so long they were tangled into a knot causing the hand to curl.

They stood in silence for what felt like twenty minutes but was likely only two. The creature then slowly turned halfway to its left, grunting twice before turning its upper body to check if Mr. Brown was still there. It repeated this action, then took a few steps away, revealing a limp. Mr. Brown described its movement as resembling an intoxicated elderly man. Behind him was a steep hill, which he believed was his only escape route considering the creature seemed to be in poor condition.

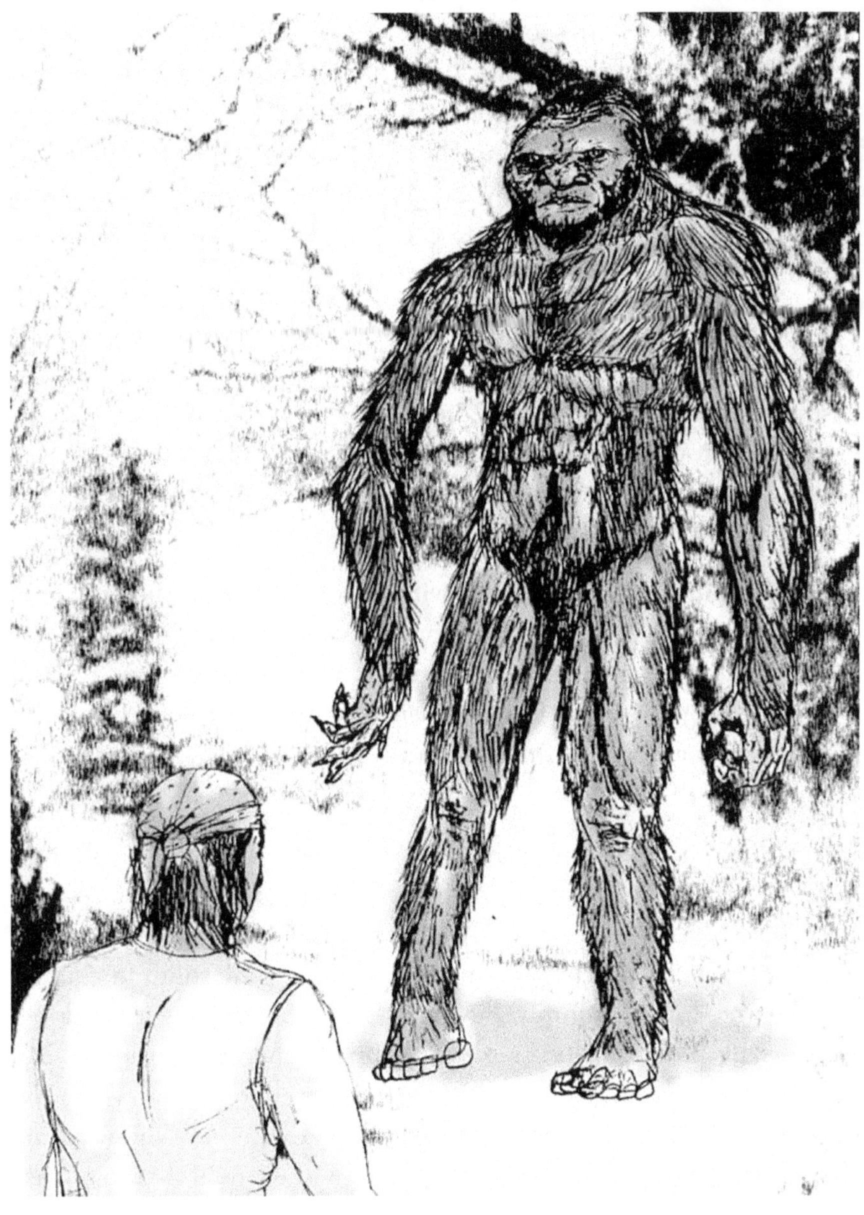

This is a drawing of what Mr. Brown claimed to have seen during his encounter. (Artist unknown)

The moment the creature moved, Mr. Brown sprinted up the hill, faster than he ever had, navigating through loose leaves, roots, and rocks. Upon reaching the top he was overcome with nausea, not from the creature's stench, but from sheer terror. On his way home, he stopped by the sheriff's office to report the incident, fearing the potential danger if the creature were to encounter a child in the forest. He also informed the local newspaper and television stations in Atlanta. Mr. Brown, who was raised to always tell the truth, felt it was his duty to warn others. While no one in Summerville has ever directly accused him of lying, he is aware that some doubt his story which has left him somewhat hurt.

That story haunted me for years. I would lie awake at night, staring into the darkness, imagining that I could hear the low growl of the Sasquatch echoing through the trees. I would imagine what it would be like to come face to face with such a creature, to look into its eyes and see an intelligence and a wildness that was both fascinating and terrifying.

As I grew older, my fascination with Sasquatch and other cryptids only increased. I devoured books on the subject, watched documentaries, and even started my own research. I would spend hours in the woods looking for signs of these elusive creatures, hoping to have my own encounter. I believe that encounter happened when I was twelve years old.

Our family had recently moved into a small rental house nestled beside an expansive cow pasture, enveloped by dense pine forests. It was a paradise for me, a sanctuary where I could lose myself in exploration and allow my imagination to roam freely. The solitude granted me the freedom to simply be myself, and so the great outdoors became my refuge. Hunting soon became a cherished pastime. My most prized possession was a BB gun that my parents had given me the previous Christmas. Perhaps some of you who have followed my show have already heard this story, but for those who haven't, what unfolded next forever altered the course of my life.

It occurred during one of my countless woodland adventures shortly after the school year had ended. I had ventured deep into unfamiliar territory, exploring an area I had never been in before. Hunting wasn't my primary focus, to be honest. On the rare occasion that I did shoot at a bird or some other creature, I would be overwhelmed with guilt afterward, so I mostly carried my BB gun for the sake of appearances. As I found myself entangled within a thicket of dense brush and towering trees, a rustling sound emanated from roughly twenty yards away. The brush was so impenetrable that visibility was limited to a mere few feet, but the noise was loud enough that I knew it had come from something substantial.

Intrigued, I stopped, trying to figure out whether it was a deer. Maybe it was a big buck or a doe accompanied by her fawn. As I stood there, listening intently, the source of the noise stopped just as quickly as it had started. Silence fell over the area, and I resumed my hike, only to realize that whatever had been shadowing me through the undergrowth had also started walking again. I stopped; it stopped. I walked; it walked. Having spent countless hours in the woods, I was familiar with the sounds of deer, raccoons, rabbits, opossums, birds, and squirrels, but this was unlike anything I had ever encountered. The footsteps were distinctly bipedal and, judging by the weighty thuds, I could tell that whatever it was, it outweighed me by several hundred pounds.

A strange sensation washed over me, causing the hair on my arms and the nape of my neck to stand on end. I had an overwhelming realization that I was trespassing in a realm where I did not belong. Paralyzed by this feeling, I stood perfectly still, while the unknown creature continued to move through the brush. Then I heard the growls, huffs, and grunts. These were not the sounds of any creature I had encountered before or since. They were deep and with a guttural intensity that sent shivers down my spine and tightened every muscle in my body. Fear gripped me and my legs became rigid. They felt like wooden posts that had been driven into the ground.

Suddenly the underbrush erupted with the sound of an elephant charging through the foliage and hurtling towards me. It stopped just beyond my line of sight, concealed within the brush. It couldn't have been more than ten feet away. Adrenaline surged through my veins, triggering my fight-or-flight response. It was a sensation I would come to experience numerous times in adulthood, but as far as I can recall, this was the first time I had felt it on this level. My primal instincts took over, and my legs regained their functionality as I quickly pivoted and ran as fast as I could in the opposite direction.

I was about six hundred yards away from our house, and I raced home with the determination that I was going to make it back to the safety of our front yard. I tore through the brush and thorns, and I refused to stop until I jumped over the barbed wire fence separating our yard from the cow pasture. Collapsing onto the grass of our front yard, I finally felt a small semblance of safety and allowed myself a moment to catch my breath. Eventually, I composed myself and made my way inside the house.

It wasn't until a few years ago that I mustered the courage to tell my mother what happened. I have never claimed, nor will I ever claim, that I had an encounter with a Sasquatch. But armed with the knowledge I have acquired over the years; I cannot help but notice the striking similarities between my experience and the countless reports shared by others. Could it have been one of these creatures that chased me out of my beloved woods?

Not knowing was simply not an option for me. I needed to know more. I wanted to share my quest for knowledge with the world and I wanted to document as many encounters with Sasquatch as possible. So, in February 2021, I started my own podcast, *Sasquatch Odyssey*.

The podcast became, and remains, a labor of love. I have dedicated countless hours to research, interviewing witnesses, and recording episodes. The response was overwhelming. Emails and messages poured in from individuals across the globe sharing their own encounters and expressing gratitude for my work. Their stories humbled and inspired me, fueling my determination to continue documenting as many Sasquatch encounters as I could.

Reflecting on it now, I realize that my fascination with Sasquatch and other cryptids went far beyond mere childhood obsession. It was a calling, a passion that has profoundly shaped my life. It has led me on a journey of discovery, not only of these elusive creatures but also of myself and my place in the world.

As I sit here in the mountains of North Carolina, far from the hills of my upbringing in north Georgia, I am still surrounded by the captivating beauty and enigma that initially ignited my fascination. I cannot help but feel immense gratitude. I am grateful for the stories passed down through generations, for the encounters shared with me, and for the opportunity to share these stories with the world.

The journey is far from complete. There are countless encounters yet to be documented, and gripping stories yet to be told. But I am prepared for the challenge. I am ready to persist in my quest, to delve deeper into the realm of Sasquatch and other cryptids, and to share my discoveries with the world.

Because, ultimately, it is not solely about the encounters themselves. It is about the stories, the experiences, the connections between us all. It is about the fascination, the mystery, the awe that is invoked. It is about the Odyssey, and I eagerly anticipate where it will lead me next.

2

THE SASQUATCH PHENOMENON

Cryptozoology, derived from the Greek words 'kryptos' meaning 'hidden', 'zoon' meaning 'animal', and 'logos' meaning 'study', is the study of hidden or unknown animals. These creatures, often referred to as cryptids, are typically species that are not recognized by the scientific community due to a lack of empirical evidence. Cryptozoology is a field that straddles the line between science and folklore, often drawing criticism and skepticism from mainstream scientists. However, it has also been responsible for the discovery of several previously unknown species, lending it a degree of credibility.

The origins of cryptozoology can be traced back to the mid-20th century, although the fascination with unknown creatures has been a part of human culture for centuries. The term 'cryptozoology' was coined by Bernard Heuvelmans, a Belgian-French zoologist, in 1955. Heuvelmans is often referred to as the 'father of cryptozoology'. He was inspired by the works of Ivan T. Sanderson, a Scottish biologist and writer who had a keen interest in unknown animals. Sanderson's 1948 book, "Abominable Snowmen: Legend Come to Life", is considered one of the foundational texts of cryptozoology.

Heuvelmans' approach to cryptozoology was scientific. He believed that the study of cryptids could lead to the discovery of new species and contribute to our understanding of biodiversity. Heuvelmans and Sanderson's work laid the foundation for cryptozoology, and their influence can still be seen in the field today.

Cryptozoology has not been fully embraced by the scientific community due to its reliance on anecdotal evidence and lack of rigorous scientific methodology. However, it has found a place in popular culture and has a dedicated following of enthusiasts and amateur researchers. Some scientists also acknowledge the potential of cryptozoology in discovering new species, as long as it adheres to scientific principles.

Cryptozoologists search for a wide range of creatures, from large, dinosaur-like beasts to small, elusive mammals. Some of the most famous cryptids include the Loch Ness Monster, Bigfoot, the Yeti, and the Chupacabra.

The Loch Ness Monster, or 'Nessie', is said to inhabit Loch Ness in the Scottish Highlands. Sightings of Nessie date back to the 6th century, but the creature gained international attention in the 1930s following several high-profile sightings. Despite numerous searches and investigations, no definitive evidence of Nessie's existence has been found.

Bigfoot is a large, hairy, bipedal creature believed to inhabit the forests of North America. Sightings of Bigfoot have been reported for centuries, and the creature has become a cultural icon. However, like Nessie, definitive proof of Bigfoot's existence remains elusive.

The Yeti, or 'Abominable Snowman', is a cryptid said to inhabit the Himalayan region of Nepal, Bhutan, and Tibet. The Yeti is often depicted as a large, ape-like creature. Despite numerous expeditions to find the Yeti, no conclusive evidence has been found.

The Chupacabra, which translates to 'goat-sucker', is a creature reported in Puerto Rico, Mexico, and the southern United States. It is said to attack livestock, particularly goats, and drain their blood. The

Chupacabra is often described as a reptile-like creature with leathery or scaly skin.

While cryptozoology is often met with skepticism, it has led to the discovery of several real animals. The okapi, a giraffe-like creature from the Democratic Republic of Congo, and the giant squid are two examples of cryptids that have been proven to exist. These discoveries demonstrate the potential value of cryptozoology and its role in expanding our understanding of the natural world.

In the world of cryptozoology, few creatures have captured the imagination and curiosity of people around the world quite like Bigfoot. Known as Sasquatch to most serious researchers, this elusive creature has become a subject of fascination, debate, and speculation for decades.

To understand the Sasquatch phenomenon, we must first explore its origins. The concept of a large, hairy humanoid creature lurking in the wilderness can be traced back to various indigenous cultures across the globe. Native American tribes, such as the Salish, Kwakiutl, and Lummi, have long shared stories of similar creatures inhabiting the dense forests of North America. These tales often depict Sasquatch as a powerful, yet elusive, guardian of the wilderness.

While skeptics may dismiss Sasquatch as nothing more than folklore, there are several compelling pieces of evidence that lend credibility to its existence.

One of the most compelling aspects of the Sasquatch phenomenon is the eyewitness account. Over the years, countless individuals claim to have encountered Sasquatch firsthand. There have been numerous reports of physical encounters with Sasquatch, including stories of individuals shooting at the creature, cars hitting it, and even literal altercations. These witnesses come from diverse backgrounds, ranging from hunters and hikers to ordinary people going about their daily lives. While these stories are difficult to verify, their descriptions consistently align. They describe a towering, bipedal creature covered in dark hair, possessing immense strength and, at times, emitting a pungent odor.

Arguably the most common and compelling piece of evidence supporting Sasquatch's existence is the discovery of footprints and trackways attributed to the creature. These tracks, often measuring between fifteen to twenty-four inches in length, exhibit a distinct mid-tarsal break, a feature not commonly found in human footprints. Numerous casts and photographs of these prints have been collected, providing tangible evidence of Sasquatch's presence. To date, I have found several such prints on our property, as well as our neighbor's place here in North Carolina.

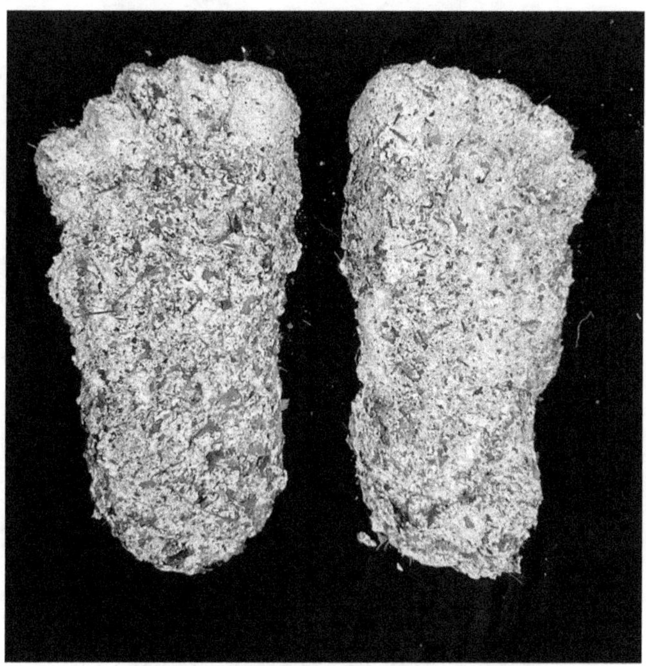

The left and right casts of prints found roughly fifty yards
from our house in October, 2023.

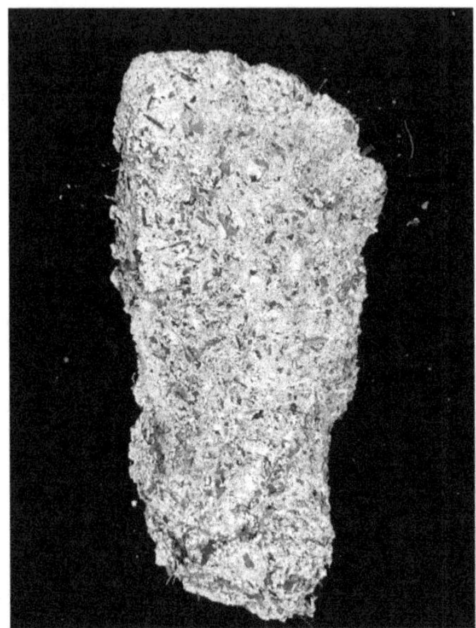

Left foot cast.

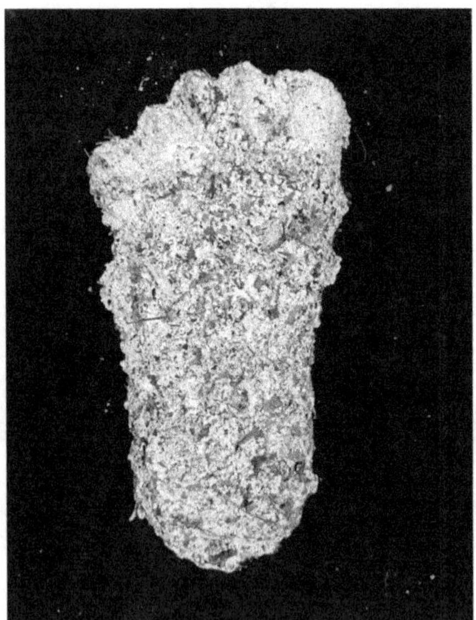

Right foot cast.

This is a photo of a single print headed up an embankment on our property.

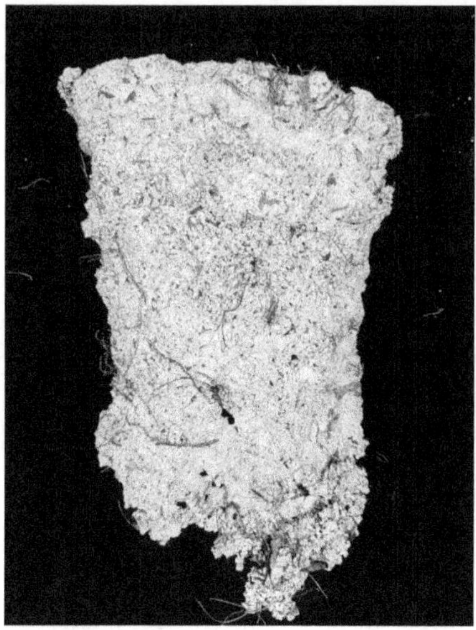

The cast of that single print you see in the previous photo.

This is a photo of a single print found on our property. This one was around a hundred and fifty yards from our house.

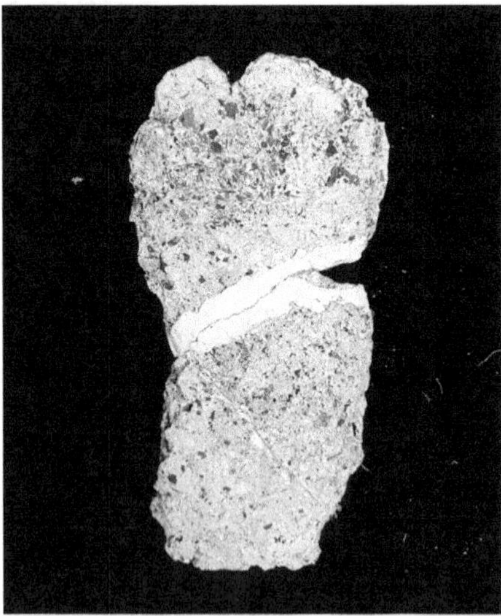

This is a cast of the print in the previous photo. You may be able to see the repairs I made after it was broken by one of my chickens.

This is a photo of a print that I found on a hike on our neighbors property, about a mile away. This was the first of two prints in a track way.

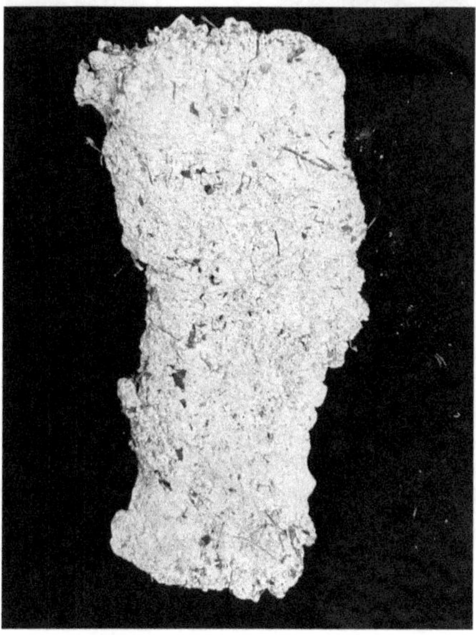

The cast of that print.

This is a photo of the first print that I found on our property during a
hike in May of 2023. Unfortunately I had no casting material and there
was more rain moving into the area, so I was unable to cast it.

Hair samples purportedly belonging to Sasquatch have been found across North America. While many of these samples have been identified as belonging to known animals, some have defied classification. These samples often resemble primate hair in their structure but do not match any known species. While contamination and insufficient quantity often hinder definitive DNA analysis, these samples add to the body of evidence suggesting the existence of a large, unknown primate.

Another intriguing aspect of the Sasquatch phenomenon is the collection of audio recordings purportedly capturing the creature's vocalizations. Known as the "Sasquatch howl" or "Bigfoot scream," these eerie sounds have been recorded in various locations, often characterized by their deep, guttural nature. While skeptics argue that these recordings could be hoaxes or misidentified animal calls, the consistency across different recordings raises questions that warrant further investigation.

The Sierra Sounds recordings, captured in the Sierra Nevada Mountains of California by Ron Morehead and Al Berry, have become a subject of intense debate within the Bigfoot community (the common name for Sasquatch researchers and believers). These recordings, analyzed by crypto linguist Scott Nelson, have been both hailed as compelling evidence of Sasquatch's existence and dismissed as an elaborate hoax.

Nelson, a former U.S. Navy officer with expertise in analyzing voice and audio recordings, has extensively studied the Sierra Sounds recordings. He argues that the vocalizations captured in the recordings exhibit linguistic patterns and complexities that are beyond the capabilities of a human hoaxer. He suggests that the range, pitch, and tonal qualities of the vocalizations are consistent with those of a large primate, supporting the idea that they are genuine Sasquatch vocalizations.

Nelson also points out the presence of subtle nuances in the recordings, such as variations in pitch, rhythm, and inflection, which he believes are indicative of a complex communication system. He argues that these characteristics are unlikely to be replicated by a human attempting to create a hoax.

Witnesses who were present during the recording sessions have provided corroborating testimony, describing the intense and visceral experience of hearing the vocalizations in person. Their accounts lend credibility to the authenticity of the recordings, as they attest to the powerful and otherworldly nature of the sounds.

Despite the arguments for authenticity, skeptics have raised several points challenging the veracity of the Sierra Sounds recordings. One of the main criticisms is the lack of visual evidence accompanying the audio. Critics argue that without visual confirmation of the source of the vocalizations, it is impossible to definitively attribute them to Sasquatch.

Some argue that the complexity and linguistic patterns identified by Scott Nelson could be the result of audio pareidolia, a psychological phenomenon where the human brain perceives patterns and meaning in random noise. They suggest that the vocalizations may be nothing more than the product of natural sounds or the creative manipulation of audio.

The absence of any corroborating physical evidence, such as footprints or hair samples, from the recording locations raises doubts about the authenticity of the recordings. Critics argue that if Sasquatch were indeed present and producing these vocalizations, there should be additional evidence to support their existence.

The debate surrounding the authenticity of the Sierra Sounds recordings continues to divide the Bigfoot community, aka Bigfoot research community. While Scott Nelson's analysis and the witness testimonies provide compelling arguments for their authenticity, skeptics raise valid concerns about the lack of visual evidence and the potential for audio manipulation.

The question of whether the Sierra Sounds recordings are genuine Sasquatch vocalizations, or an elaborate hoax remains unanswered. As the search for conclusive evidence of Sasquatch's existence continues, these recordings serve as a reminder of the complexities and challenges inherent in unraveling the truth concerning the existence of Sasquatch.

The Patterson-Gimlin film, shot on October 20, 1967, in Bluff Creek, California, remains one of the most compelling pieces of video evidence in the quest to prove the existence of Sasquatch. The film was shot by Roger Patterson and Bob Gimlin, two men who had set out specifically to capture footage for their documentary film about Sasquatch.

The film shot on a 16mm camera, lasts for just under one minute and depicts a large, hairy bipedal creature walking along the creek bed. The creature, which has come to be known as "Patty," is estimated to be about seven feet tall, with a weight of approximately seven hundred pounds. The film shows the creature walking away from the camera, turning to look at the men briefly before disappearing into the woods.

The film has been subjected to numerous analyses over the years. Anthropologists, primatologists, and special effects experts have all scrutinized the footage. Some argue that the creature's movements are too fluid and natural to be a man in a suit, while others point to the muscle definition visible beneath the fur as evidence of its authenticity. However, skeptics claim that the film could be an elaborate hoax, pointing to inconsistencies in Patterson and Gimlin's accounts of the event.

The Paul Freeman footage, shot in the Blue Mountains of Washington State in 1992, is another significant piece of video evidence in the Sasquatch research. Freeman, a former U.S. Forest Service patrolman, had reported multiple Sasquatch sightings since the 1980s, but it was this footage that brought him into the limelight.

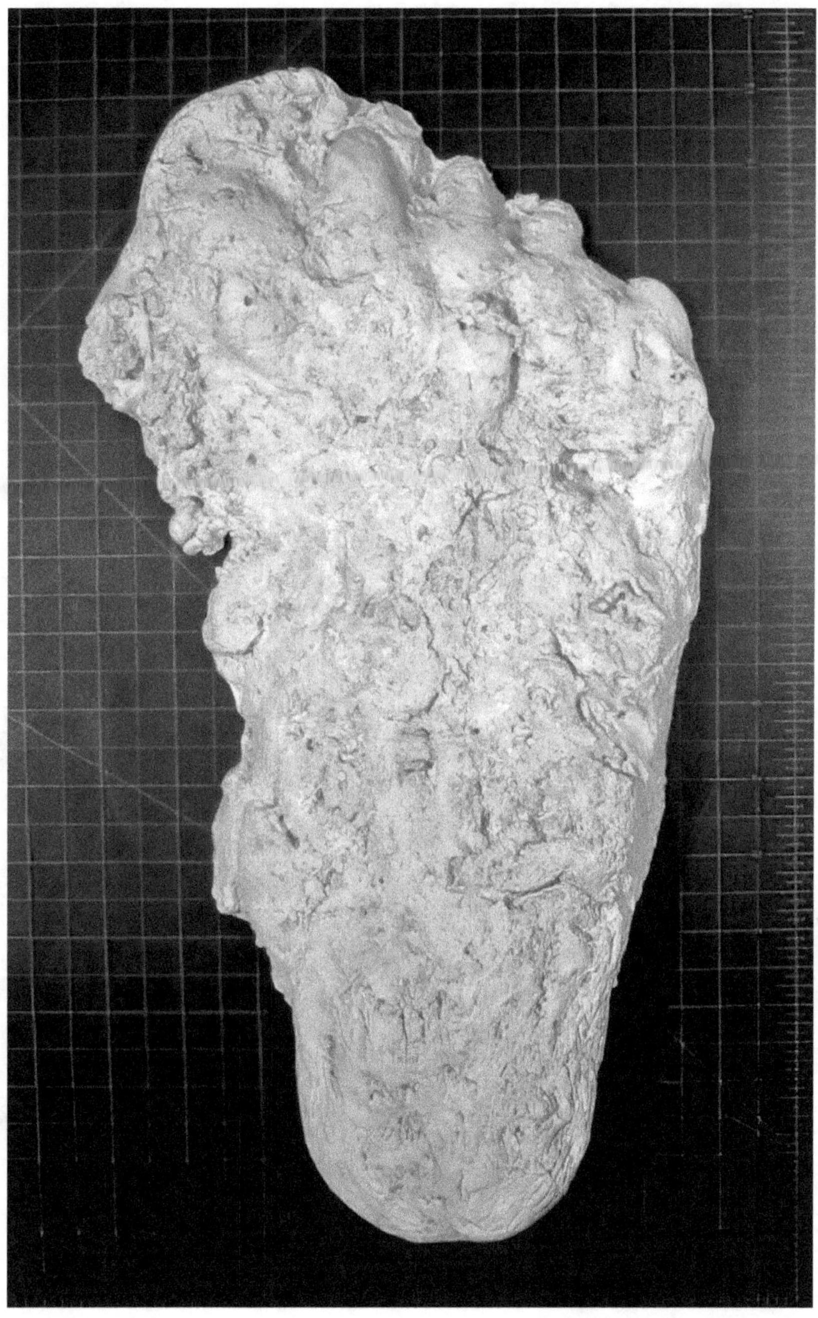

The Paul Freeman dermal ridges. June 16th, 1982. Found at Elk Wallow in Low Canyon. 15 inches. Left foot. Photo courtesy of Michael Freeman.

Paul Freeman in the Blue mountains, 1987. Examining
tree break. Photo courtesy of Michael Freeman.

Paul Freeman in the early 1990's, examining a possible bed in the Blue
Mountains. Photo courtesy of Michael Freeman.

Paul Freeman, August 21st, 1992. Deduct Spring, Oregon. Casting tracks with Wes Sumerlin from the Freeman Footage encounter of August 20. Photo courtesy of Michael Freeman.

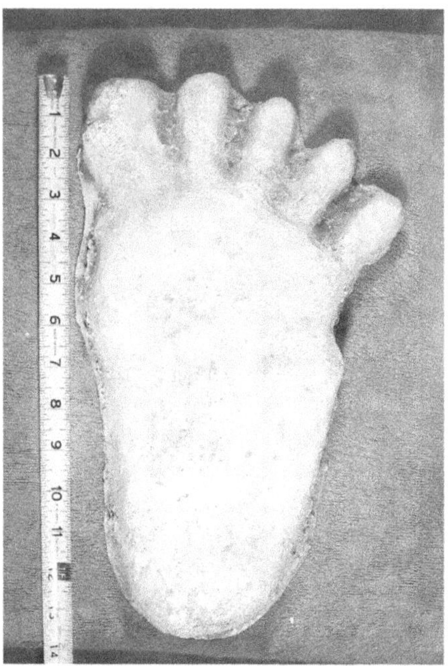

Wrinkle Foot. Found at Table Springs in 1984. 14 inches.
Left foot. Photo courtesy of Michael Freeman.

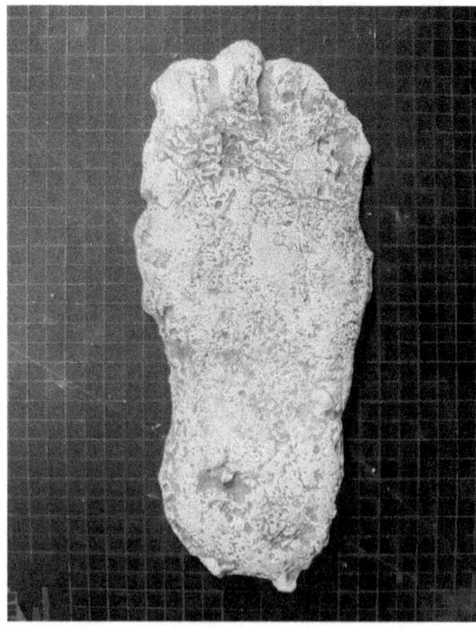

January 14th, 1991. Mill Creek Road. The seven mile
tracks. 13.5 inches. Left foot. Photo courtesy of Michael
Freeman.

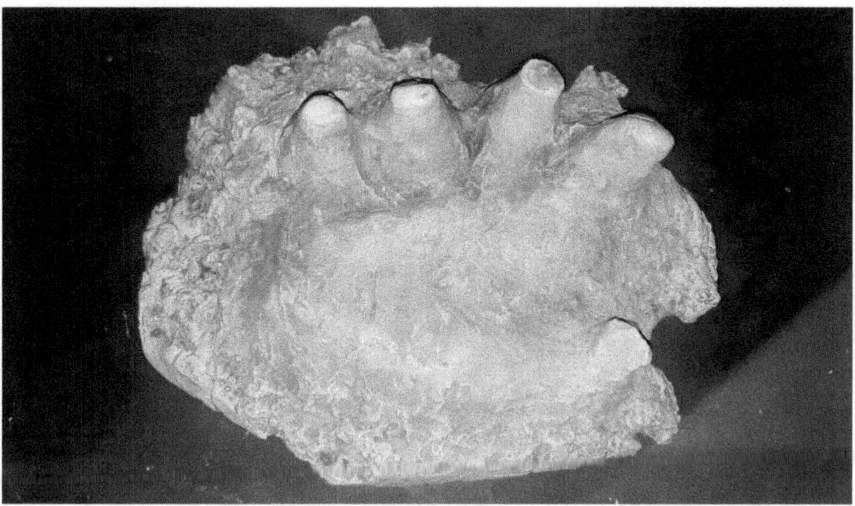

Right hand. Found on Biscuit Ridge, Blue Mountains, 1994. 8.5 inches across palm. Photo courtesy of Michael Freeman.

The footage, shot on a handheld video camera, shows a large, hairy creature walking through the woods. The creature appears to be aware of Freeman's presence, as it frequently looks towards the camera. The video also shows what appears to be a juvenile Sasquatch following the larger creature.

The Freeman footage has been subjected to similar scrutiny as the Patterson-Gimlin film. Some experts argue that the creature's movements and the footprints found at the site suggest that it could be a genuine Sasquatch. However, skeptics point to Freeman's history of Sasquatch sightings and question the authenticity of the footage.

Both the Patterson-Gimlin film and the Paul Freeman footage have played significant roles in the ongoing debate about the existence of Sasquatch. While neither piece of evidence has been definitively proven or disproven, they continue to fuel the fascination and intrigue surrounding the creature.

The Skookum cast is a plaster mold showcasing what appears to be a large creature's left forearm, hip, thigh, and buttocks. The imprint was discovered in a muddy wallow near Mount Adams in Washington state's southern region in 2000. Some speculate that the imprint was left by Sasquatch. The cast was made on September 22, 2000, during a Bigfoot Field Researchers Organization (BFRO) expedition to the Skookum Meadows area of the Gifford Pinchot National Forest, coinciding with the filming of the *Animal X* television show. The researchers left the fruit in the muddy wallow overnight and the impression was discovered the following morning.

The cast, which measures 3.5 by 5 feet and weighs approximately 400 pounds, is a partial body imprint left in the mud by the roadside. As depicted in the *Animal X* episode, the Skookum cast was digitally scanned for further study and was also inspected by physical anthropologist Dr. Grover Krantz, wildlife biologist Dr. John Bindernagel, and others. Dr. Krantz voiced his belief that the cast was made by a Sasquatch, while others remain skeptical. Dr. Jeffrey Meldrum, a professor in the Department of Anthropology at Idaho State University, also inspected the cast. He identified specific details in what he believed to be the foot area of the cast and found evidence of dermatoglyphics that he thought were related to primate feet.

The Committee for Skeptical Inquiry proposed that the initial identification was rushed and influenced subsequent team members. The cast was created by wildlife ecologist LeRoy Fish, tracker Richard Noll, and animal tracker Derek Randles. During their search for Sasquatch evidence, Richard Noll noticed the impression and suggested to his team that it was left by a Sasquatch. This suggestion may have swayed the team members, leading them to confirm the original identification. Here is the official press release from Idaho State University addressing the Skookum Cast. The statement was written by Glenn Alford and released on October 23, 2000.

Pocatello – Dr. Jeff Meldrum, associate professor of anatomy and anthropology at Idaho State University, is a member of the scientific team examining a plaster cast of what may be the first documented body imprint of a Sasquatch.

The imprint of what appears to be a large animal's left forearm, hip, thigh, and heel was discovered Sept. 22 in a muddy wallow near Mt. Adams in southern Washington state by a Bigfoot Field Researchers Organization (www.BFRO.net) expedition in the Gifford Pinchot National Forest.

The investigating team, including Meldrum; Dr. Grover Krantz, a retired physical anthropologist from Washington State University; Dr. John Bindernagel, Canadian wildlife biologist; John Green, a retired Canadian journalist, and author; and Dr. Ron Brown, an exotic animal handler and health care administrator, all examined the cast and agreed that it cannot be attributed to any commonly known Northwest animal and may represent an unknown primate.

Meldrum, whose research includes comparative primate anatomy, and the emergence of human walking, supervised the careful cleaning of the cast and will coordinate its analysis by a scientific team. He first became actively interested in the question of the existence of a North American ape after examining fresh Sasquatch tracks in 1996.

While not definitively proving the existence of a species of North American ape, the cast constitutes significant and compelling new evidence that will hopefully stimulate further serious research and investigation into the presence of these primates in the Northwest mountains and elsewhere," Meldrum said.

Dr. LeRoy Fish, a retired wildlife ecologist from Triangles Lake, Ore., with a doctorate in zoology from Washington State University; Derek Randles, a landscape architect from Belfair, Wash.; and Richard Noll, a tooling metrologist from Edmonds, Wash.; discovered and cast the partial body imprint during the BFRO expedition.

More than 200 pounds of plaster were needed to produce the 3-1/2 x 5-foot cast of the entire impression, which was reinforced with researchers' aluminum tent poles. Other Sasquatch evidence documented by the BFRO expedition includes voice recordings and indistinct 17-inch footprints.

Trace evidence attributed to Sasquatch is usually footprints, but impressions of other body parts, including hands, knuckles, and buttocks, have occasionally been found. This unique instance of a partial body impression provides further insights into this elusive ape species' anatomy. Preliminary measurements indicate its body dimensions are 40 to 50 percent greater than those of a six-foot-tall human.

After the cast was cleaned, extensive impressions of hair on the buttock and thigh surfaces and a fringe of longer hair along the forearm were evident. Meldrum identified what appear to be skin ridge patterns on the heel, comparable to fingerprints, which are characteristic of primates.

The ridge characteristics are consistent with other examples from Sasquatch footprints Meldrum has studied in collaboration with Officer Jimmy Chilcutt, a latent fingerprint examiner with the Conroe, Texas, Police Department. The anatomy of the heel, ankle, and Achilles tendon are also distinct and consistent with models of the Sasquatch foot derived by Meldrum after examining hundreds of alleged Sasquatch footprints.

Hair samples collected at the scene and from the cast itself and examined by Dr. Henner Fahrenbach, a biomedical research scientist from Beaverton, Ore., were primarily of deer, elk, coyote, and bear, as was expected since tracks in the wallow were mostly of those animals. However, based on characteristics matching those of otherwise indeterminate primate hairs collected in association with other Sasquatch sightings, he identified a single distinctly primate hair as 'Sasquatch.

Sasquatch is a species of North American ape suspected to inhabit the mountainous forests of the Northwest. Its existence remains controversial despite numerous eyewitness sightings and the discovery of enormous footprints.

More information about the Skookum Cast can be found at the website for the Bigfoot Field Researchers Organization: http://www.bfro.net

We certainly can't talk about evidence of Sasquatch's existence without including "tree breaks" and "stick structures". Tree breaks are trees or large branches that have been snapped or twisted at a height that would be difficult for a human to reach without the aid of tools or machinery. The breaks are often clean, suggesting a significant amount of force was used. Some researchers argue that these breaks are directional markers or territorial signs made by Sasquatch.

It's important to note that tree breaks can occur naturally due to weather conditions such as wind, snow, or ice. Animals like bears or moose can also cause similar damage while foraging for food. Therefore, while tree breaks can be intriguing, they are not definitive proof of Sasquatch's existence.

This is an interesting collection of smaller sticks on top of a large log that we found on a hike of the property. You may notice that the top stick is balanced on top of the others.

Dani and I came upon this captivating structure resembling a "tee pee" on our neighbor's land, just a few hundred yards from where we had discovered, photographed, and cast the two prints featured earlier in this chapter.

Stick structures, on the other hand, are formations of sticks and branches that are arranged in a way that appears intentional and beyond the capabilities of natural forces. These structures can take various forms, including teepees, arches, and X-shapes. Some are quite large and complex, suggesting a level of intelligence and physical ability beyond that of known animals.

Critics of the Sasquatch theory argue that these structures could be the work of humans, either as part of outdoor activities or as deliberate hoaxes. However, many of these structures are found in remote areas, far from human habitation or common hiking trails, which makes the human explanation less likely.

While tree beaks and stick structures provide intriguing evidence for the existence of Sasquatch, they are not definitive proof. Both phenomena can have natural or human explanations. That said, the consistent patterns, the remote locations, and the sheer physical force required to create these signs suggest that they should not be dismissed outright. Further research is needed to determine their true origin and significance.

While Sasquatch researchers continue to speculate about tree breaks or stick structures, we know for a fact that known apes do use trees and foliage.

Nest building is a common behavior among great apes, including orangutans, gorillas, bonobos, and chimpanzees. These nests serve various purposes such as providing a safe place for rest and sleep, protecting against predators, and offering comfort during harsh weather conditions. The process of nest building involves complex cognitive skills and physical abilities, highlighting the intelligence and adaptability of this species.

The primary reason for nest building in great apes is to provide a safe and comfortable place for rest and sleep. For instance, orangutans in Borneo and Sumatra build elaborate nests high in the canopy to avoid ground-based predators. These nests are often lined with soft leaves and branches for added comfort, demonstrating a level of foresight and planning.

The techniques used in nest building vary among species and individuals, reflecting the adaptability and learning capabilities of great apes. Chimpanzees, for example, have been observed using a variety of materials and techniques in their nest construction, including weaving branches together, bending larger branches into a supportive structure, and even using stones and other non-vegetative materials.

The complexity of nest building in great apes also provides insights into their social structure and communication skills. Gorillas, for instance, often build their nests in close proximity to each other, suggesting a level of social cohesion and mutual protection. Furthermore, the act of nest building is often a learned behavior, passed down from mothers to their offspring, indicating a form of cultural transmission.

The behavior of nest building in great apes is a complex process that serves multiple purposes, from providing safety and comfort to facilitating social cohesion. The techniques used in nest construction highlight the cognitive abilities and adaptability of these species, while the social aspects of this behavior provide insights into their communication skills and social structure. As such, the study of nest building in great apes not only enhances our understanding of these fascinating creatures but also sheds light on the evolutionary origins of human intelligence and culture.

Building behaviors in great apes, particularly in species like orangutans, gorillas, and chimpanzees, are well-documented and studied. These primates are known to construct complex structures for various purposes, such as nests for sleeping, platforms for feeding, and even tools for foraging. The structures they build are often intricate and purposeful, demonstrating a high level of cognitive ability and manual dexterity.

In comparison, Sasquatch research, which is largely speculative due to the lack of concrete evidence of the creature's existence, often cites stick structures and tree breaks as potential signs of Sasquatch activity. These structures are typically described as large, seemingly unnatural arrangements of branches and trees, often in remote areas. Tree breaks, in particular, are often interpreted as territorial markers or directional signs.

This is an interesting collection of photos of what appears to be possible nest like structures.

When comparing the two, it is important to consider the differences in context and evidence. Great ape building behaviors are based on direct observation and study, while Sasquatch-related structures are largely based on conjecture and interpretation. If we were to assume the existence of Sasquatches for the sake of comparison, we could draw some parallels and contrasts.

Both great apes and the hypothetical Sasquatches seem to use available materials in their environment to construct structures, demonstrating a level of environmental awareness and problem-solving ability. However, the complexity and purpose of the structures differ. Great apes build nests for specific, immediate needs like sleeping or eating. Sasquatch structures, on the other hand, are theorized to serve more abstract purposes like communication or territory marking.

The physical strength required to create these structures may also be a point of comparison. Great apes, while strong, are limited by their size and physical capabilities. The size and weight of the materials used in Sasquatch structures, if they are indeed created by such a creature, would suggest a significantly larger and stronger animal.

While there are some potential similarities in the building behaviors of great apes and the hypothesized Sasquatch, there are also significant differences, primarily in the complexity, purpose, and physical requirements of the structures. Without concrete evidence and direct observation of Sasquatches, these comparisons remain largely speculative.

Alongside what many consider to be the facts, Sasquatch has also become entangled in a web of myths and misconceptions. These myths often arise from sensationalized media portrayals, hoaxes, and misinterpretations. Let's explore some of the most prevalent myths and misconceptions surrounding Sasquatch.

There are some in the community that suggest that Sasquatch possesses supernatural abilities, such as the power to disappear or become invisible at will. While these claims may add an air of mystery to the creature, there is no concrete evidence to support such extraordinary abilities. Generally, the Bigfoot community is divided into two main camps: those who believe Sasquatch is a physical, flesh-and-blood creature, and those who subscribe to the theory of 'high strangeness,' suggesting Sasquatch is a supernatural or inter-dimensional being. I believe that to fully understand this enigma, we must look at the intricacies of both arguments, exploring the evidence and theories that support each perspective.

The high strangeness theory posits that Sasquatch is a supernatural or inter-dimensional entity. This theory is often supported by the lack of physical evidence, such as a carcass or bones, despite numerous sightings. Proponents of this theory often cite accounts of Sasquatch disappearing inexplicably, glowing eyes, telepathic communication, and its association with other paranormal phenomena like UFOs or UAPs.

The high strangeness theory also draws upon Native American folk-lore, where creatures resembling Sasquatch, such as the Wendigo, are often depicted as spiritual beings or shapeshifters. Some argue that the creature's elusive nature and the strange circumstances surrounding many sightings suggest a being that exists outside of our conventional understanding of biology and physics.

While there are many that subscribe to the high strangeness aspect of the mystery, the flesh-and-blood proponents argue that Sasquatch t is a yet-to-be-discovered primate, possibly a relic hominid or a descendant of *Gigantopithecus*, an extinct genus of ape. This theory is supported by the physical evidence collected over the years, including footprints, hair samples, and the famous Patterson-Gimlin film.

It is difficult to have a conversation with anyone about Sasquatch without talking about what these creatures could be. If they are in fact some sort of giant, bipedal, ape, then where do they fall on our bushy family tree? I have heard many speculate about what these creatures are and how closely related to humans they may or may not be. In my own research, I have narrowed the list of potential suspects to two known extinct ape species.

The first and most likely candidate for Sasquatch should they exist, in my opinion, is the aforementioned *Gigantopithecus*. *Gigantopithecus*, often referred to as the "giant ape," is an extinct genus of primates that lived during the Pleistocene, approximately nine million to one hundred thousand years ago. This fascinating creature is known for its enormous size, making it the largest primate to have ever existed. While our knowledge of *Gigantopithecus* is limited due to the scarcity of fossil remains, paleontologists have pieced together some information about its origins, characteristics, and place in the fossil record.

Gigantopithecus is believed to have originated in what is now Southeast Asia, specifically in regions that encompass modern-day China, India, and Vietnam. The genus likely evolved from smaller primates, possibly from the family Hominidae, which includes humans, orangutans, gorillas, and chimpanzees. The exact evolutionary relationship between *Gigantopithecus* and other primates remains uncertain due to the scarcity of fossil evidence.

Based on the limited fossil remains discovered, scientists estimate that *Gigantopithecus* stood approximately ten feet tall and weighed around eleven and twelve hundred pounds, making it significantly larger than any living primate. Its massive size suggests that it was an herbivorous creature, relying on a diet of plants, fruits, and bamboo. The structure of its jaw and teeth indicates that it had a robust chewing apparatus, enabling it to process tough vegetation.

The fossil record of *Gigantopithecus* is quite sparse, consisting primarily of teeth and jaw fragments. These remains have been found in various locations across Southeast Asia, including China, Vietnam, and India. The majority of the fossils were discovered in cave deposits, where the conditions were favorable for preservation. However, due to the scarcity of skeletal remains, reconstructing the complete anatomy and behavior of *Gigantopithecus* remains challenging.

The first *Gigantopithecus* fossils were discovered in 1935 when a paleontologist named Ralph von Koenigswald found several large teeth in a Chinese pharmacy. These teeth were initially mistaken for those of an extinct species of giant orangutan. Subsequent discoveries of additional teeth and jaw fragments helped scientists understand the immense size and unique characteristics of this ancient primate.

Gigantopithecus' place in the fossil record provides valuable insights into the evolutionary history of primates. Its existence demonstrates the diversity of primates during the Pleistocene epoch and highlights the potential for gigantism in certain lineages. However, due to the limited fossil evidence, many questions about *Gigantopithecus* remain unanswered, such as its locomotion, social behavior, and the reasons for its eventual extinction.

Gigantopithecus with its massive size and herbivorous diet, occupied a unique ecological niche. While our understanding of this fascinating creature is limited, the discovery of its fossil remains has provided valuable insights into the evolutionary history of primates and the potential for gigantism in certain lineages. If some of these giant creatures made their way into North America and somehow managed to survive into the present day, they could very well be what many have described in countless encounter stories as the giants we refer to as Sasquatch or Bigfoot.

The second least likely on my Sasquatch suspect list is *Australopithecus*. They are a genus of extinct hominins that lived in Africa between 4.2 and 1.9 million years ago. They are considered to be the earliest known hominins or human ancestors and played a crucial role in our understanding of human evolution. The genus *Australopithecus* includes several species, the most famous of which are *Australopithecus afarensis* and *Australopithecus africanus*.

The story of *Australopithecus* begins around seven million years ago when the common ancestor of humans and chimpanzees lived in Africa. Over time, this lineage diverged, and around 4.2 million years ago, the first *Australopithecus* species emerged. These early *Australopithecines* were bipedal, meaning they walked on two legs but still retained some ape-like features.

The most well-known species is *Australopithecus afarensis*, which lived between 3.9 and 2.9 million years ago. The most famous individual of this species is "Lucy," a nearly complete skeleton discovered in Ethiopia in 1974. Lucy provided valuable insights into the anatomy and locomotion of *Australopithecus afarensis*. This species had a small brain, a projecting face, and a combination of ape-like and human-like features. They were likely arboreal, spending time in trees, but also capable of walking on two legs on the ground.

Another significant *Australopithecus* species is *Australopithecus africanus*, which lived between three and two million years ago. Fossils of this species were first discovered in South Africa in the early 20th century. *Australopithecus africanus* had a more human-like face and teeth compared to *Australopithecus afarensis*. They also had a slightly larger brain size and were likely more terrestrial than their predecessors.

The fossil record of *Australopithecus* is primarily based on skeletal remains, including skulls, teeth, and post-cranial bones. These fossils have provided valuable information about their anatomy, behavior, and evolutionary relationships. Additionally, the discovery of stone tools associated with *Australopithecus afarensis* suggests that they had some level of tool use, although their capabilities were likely limited compared to later hominin species.

The *Australopithecus* species gradually gave rise to the genus *Homo*, which includes modern humans. The exact relationship between *Australopithecus* and *Homo* is still a topic of debate among scientists. Some propose that *Australopithecus afarensis* is a direct ancestor of *Homo*, while others suggest that they represent a side branch in our evolutionary tree.

Australopithecus represents a crucial stage in human evolution. They were the earliest known hominins and played a significant role in the transition from ape-like ancestors to the genus *Homo*. Through their fossils, we have gained valuable insights into the origins of bipedalism, tool use, and other key characteristics that define our species. Early on in my research into the possible candidates for Sasquatch in the known fossil record, I strongly believed that *Australopithecus* could be what many people encounter here in North America and many other places around the world. It may still be a viable candidate, so it remains on my very short list of known apes in the fossil record.

We may never know exactly what Sasquatch are, but there is one thing we can say for sure. Many people are finding large footprints, often measuring fifteen to twenty-four inches in length, and exhibiting dermal ridges, sweat pores, and other primate characteristics. One of the most well-known incidents occurred in the small town of Bossburg, Washington, on November 24, 1969. It all began when peculiar tracks resembling those of a human, but with a visibly injured right foot, were discovered near the local dump. The discovery came shortly after a woman had reported a sighting of a Sasquatch in the vicinity. Locals quickly dubbed the track maker the "Bossburg Cripple," but it later became known as "Cripplefoot."

News of the tracks spread like wildfire, attracting the attention of renowned Sasquatch researcher, René Dahinden. However, upon his arrival on November 27, he found that the tracks had been mostly trampled by curious onlookers. Determined to gather evidence, Dahinden managed to photograph and cast the best print he could find. Another dedicated searcher, Bob Titmus, joined him for three days, and later returned a month later to continue the investigation.

After an arduous two-week search, Sasquatch enthusiasts Ivan Marx and René Dahinden finally stumbled upon a breakthrough on December 13, 1969. They uncovered an astonishing 1,089 enormous human-like tracks in the snow, leading to and from a river near Lake Roosevelt, close to Bossburg. The discovery prompted anthropologist Grover Krantz to join them, capturing photographs and creating casts of the tracks. Not long after, renowned Patterson filmmaker Roger Patterson and his assistant, Dennis Jenson, dedicated themselves full-time to the investigation.

The casts and photographs of the tracks were later examined by esteemed primatologist John Napier and anthropologist Jeff Meldrum, both of whom became convinced of their authenticity. René Dahinden, although initially skeptical due to certain circumstances, was also impressed by the tracks. He couldn't help but question the timing of the discovery, as his companion, Ivan Marx, had mysteriously pulled over and left the vehicle just before stumbling upon the tracks. Dahinden suspected that the occupants of an empty Jeep parked nearby may have been involved in creating the tracks. However, despite his suspicions, Dahinden ultimately accepted the tracks as genuine evidence.

The Bossburg Cripple and the multitude of tracks near Lake Roosevelt had ignited a fervor among researchers and scientists alike. The quest to uncover the truth behind these enigmatic footprints continued, leaving an indelible mark on the history of Sasquatch exploration.

Interestingly, some researchers propose a hybrid theory, suggesting that Sasquatch could be a physical creature with paranormal abilities, bridging the gap between the flesh-and-blood and high strangeness theories. This theory, while controversial, reflects the complexity and ongoing mystery of the Sasquatch phenomenon.

The debate between the flesh-and-blood and high strangeness theories represents the heart of the Bigfoot community's quest for understanding. Both theories, while seemingly at odds, reflect a shared desire to unravel the mystery of Sasquatch, whether it be a creature of our physical world or a being from beyond our current comprehension.

The question of whether Sasquatch is real remains unanswered definitively. While skeptics argue that the lack of concrete scientific evidence dismisses its existence, the accumulation of eyewitness accounts, footprints, and audio recordings cannot be easily disregarded. The question of whether or not Sasquatch exists continues to captivate the imaginations of many, inspiring further research and exploration into the unknown corners of our world. Whether Sasquatch is a flesh-and-blood creature or a product of folklore and misidentification, the legend persists, reminding us of the enduring allure of the unknown.

3

SASQUATCH HISTORY

The best predictor of the future is often the past. I have always been fascinated by the history of Sasquatch reports that predate the sensationalizing of the subject. That said, let's take a look at some of the historical accounts and eyewitness testimonies that have shaped the enduring legend of Sasquatch.

From ancient indigenous folklore to modern-day encounters, the presence of this elusive creature has left an indelible mark on human history. As we explore some of the most compelling and well-documented instances of Sasquatch sightings, we can begin to get a more comprehensive overview of the historical record.

Long before European settlers arrived in North America, indigenous tribes across the continent had a deep-rooted connection with the land and its inhabitants. Sasquatch, Bigfoot, Skookum, or *Ts'emekwes*, played a significant role in the folklore and traditions of Native American and First Nations cultures. In this chapter, we will explore the rich tapestry of Sasquatch legends and beliefs, highlighting the diverse accounts and historical significance within different tribes.

The Salish tribes, including the Coast Salish, Interior Salish, and Salishan-speaking peoples, have a long-standing relationship with Sasquatch. According to their oral traditions, Sasquatch is known as *Sásq'ets* or *Sasq'etsa*, a powerful and elusive creature that inhabits dense forests and mountains.

The Salish people believe that Sasquatch possesses supernatural abilities and is often associated with spiritual guardianship. They view encounters with Sasquatch as a sign of good fortune or a warning to respect the natural world. These stories have been passed down through generations, serving as a reminder of the interconnectedness between humans and the wilderness.

The Kwakiutl and Nuu-chah-nulth tribes, located in the Pacific Northwest, also have a rich history of Sasquatch legends. Known as *Bukwus* or *Dzunukwa*, Sasquatch is often depicted as a wild and hairy creature, associated with the spirit world and the supernatural.

In Kwakiutl mythology, *Bukwus* is believed to be a guardian of the forest, responsible for maintaining the balance between humans and nature. The Nuu-chah-nulth people, on the other hand, view *Dzunukwa* as a fearsome and powerful being, associated with the harvest and fertility.

The Chehalis tribe, located in the Pacific Northwest, has a unique perspective on Sasquatch. According to their oral traditions, Sasquatch is known as *Skookum* or "Stick Indians." The Chehalis people believe that Skookum is a mischievous and elusive creature, often associated with the deep forests and mountains.

Skookum is said to possess great strength and intelligence, capable of outwitting humans. The Chehalis people view encounters with Skookum as a test of one's courage and respect for the natural world. They caution against venturing too deep into the wilderness, as it is believed to be the domain of Skookum.

The Lummi tribe, located in the Pacific Northwest, has a unique perspective on Sasquatch. According to their oral traditions,

Sasquatch is known as *Ts'emekwes*, a giant, hairy being that inhabits the dense forests. Ts'emekwes is often depicted as a guardian of the wilderness, responsible for maintaining the balance between humans and nature. The Lummi people believe that encounters with Ts'emekwes serve as a reminder to respect the land and its inhabitants.

Numerous other Native American and First Nations tribes have their own Sasquatch legends and beliefs. The Haida people of the Pacific Northwest, for example, have stories of *Gogit* or *Guguyni*, a creature similar to Sasquatch. The Sts'ailes people of British Columbia speak of *Sasq'ets*, a creature associated with the mountains and forests.

These accounts highlight the widespread presence of Sasquatch in indigenous cultures, emphasizing the deep reverence and respect for the natural world. Sasquatch is often seen as a guardian or spiritual being, reminding humans of their interconnectedness with the land and the importance of living in harmony with nature.

The Native American and First Nations history of Sasquatch is a testament to the deep-rooted connection between indigenous cultures and the natural world. Sasquatch, known by various names and depicted in diverse ways, holds a significant place in the folklore and traditions of tribes across North America.

These legends serve as a reminder of the importance of respecting and preserving the wilderness, as well as the spiritual significance of our relationship with the land. The sheer number of Sasquatch stories within Native American and First Nations history adds depth and cultural context to the enduring mystery of Sasquatch.

The Native Americans were not the only ones to have experiences with large, hairy bipedal creatures. As European explorers and settlers ventured into the uncharted territories of North America, they encountered a vast and unfamiliar wilderness teeming with mysterious creatures. Among these encounters were reports of large, hairy beings that closely resembled the legendary Sasquatch. In this chapter, we will delve into the accounts of early European explorers and settlers who claimed to have encountered these enigmatic creatures, shedding light on their experiences and the impact these encounters had on their understanding of the New World.

David Thompson Encounter

David Thompson, a renowned British-Canadian explorer and cartographer, is among the first European explorers to document an encounter with a Sasquatch-like creature. In 1811, while traversing the Rocky Mountains near Jasper, Alberta, Thompson and his party came across a set of enormous footprints in the snow. The tracks measured around fourteen inches in length and were spaced far apart, indicating a creature of considerable size.

Thompson's Indigenous guides informed him that these footprints belonged to a creature known as "Old Man of the Woods" or "Big Foot." They described it as a large, hairy being that inhabited the mountains and forests. Although Thompson did not personally witness the creature, the footprints left an indelible impression on him, sparking his curiosity and leaving him with a lasting belief in the existence of such creatures.

Another notable encounter occurred in 1793 when Scottish explorer Alexander Mackenzie embarked on an expedition to find a route to the Pacific Ocean. While exploring the Bella Coola region of British Columbia, Mackenzie and his party encountered a group of Indigenous people who shared stories of a creature they called *Matlox*.

According to the Indigenous accounts, Matlox was a large, hairy creature that resembled a man but possessed incredible strength and agility. The locals warned Mackenzie to be cautious and avoid the creature's territory. Although Mackenzie did not personally encounter Matlox, the stories he heard left a lasting impression on him and added to the growing body of evidence suggesting the presence of Sasquatch-like beings in the region.

Settler Accounts

As European settlers began to establish communities in North America, they too encountered strange and inexplicable creatures that resembled Sasquatch. In the early 19th century, settlers in the Pacific Northwest reported sightings of large, hairy beings lurking in the forests.

One such account comes from the Hudson's Bay Company fur trader John Work, who documented an encounter in 1811. While stationed at a trading post near present-day Tête Jaune Cache, British Columbia, Work and his men observed a large, hairy creature from a distance. The creature was described as standing upright and moving with a human-like gait. Although Work did not approach the creature, the sighting left him and his companions in awe and fueled their curiosity about the wilderness they inhabited.

The encounters of early European explorers and settlers with Sasquatch-like creatures in North America provide intriguing glimpses into the rich tapestry of legends and folklore surrounding these enigmatic beings. From David Thompson's discovery of massive footprints to Alexander Mackenzie's encounters with Indigenous accounts, these encounters left a lasting impact on the explorers and settlers, challenging their understanding of the New World and igniting their curiosity about the creatures that inhabited its vast wilderness.

The Bauman Incident

Among the many accounts that have emerged over the years, one story stands out as a cornerstone in the Sasquatch lore - the infamous Bauman Bigfoot story.

Within the pages of Theodore Roosevelt's book, *The Wilderness Hunter*, lies a riveting account that has both fascinated and perplexed enthusiasts for over a century. Published in 1893, Roosevelt's memoir chronicles his adventures in the untamed wilderness of the American West, where he encountered not only the beauty of nature but also the enigmatic presence of the Bauman Bigfoot.

Roosevelt's vivid descriptions and meticulous attention to detail carry us back in time to a realm of mystery and untold wonders. Through his words, we are transported to the dense forests of the Bitterroot Mountains, where the encounter with the Bauman Bigfoot forever etched itself into the annals of cryptozoology.

The Bauman Bigfoot story begins with the tale of two seasoned trappers, Bauman and his companion, who ventured deep into the heart of the wilderness in search of beaver pelts. Little did they know that their expedition would soon take an unexpected turn.

Roosevelt's account of the Bauman Bigfoot is not merely a retelling of a mysterious encounter; it is a testament to the enduring allure of the unknown. It serves as a reminder that even in the age of science and reason, there are still creatures that elude our understanding, lurking in the shadows of our collective consciousness.

Here is the Bauman story as it appeared in Roosevelt's book.

> Frontiersmen are not, as a rule, apt to be superstitious. They lead lives too hard and practical, and have too little imagination in things spiritual and supernatural. I have heard but few ghost stories while living on the frontier, and those few were of a perfectly commonplace and conventional type.
>
> But I once listened to a goblin story, which rather impressed me. A grizzled, weather-beaten old mountain hunter, by the name of Bauman, who was born and had passed all his life on the frontier. He must have believed what he said, for he could hardly repress a shudder at a certain point of the tale; but he was of German ancestry, and in childhood had doubtless been saturated with all kinds of ghost and goblin lore, so that many fearsome superstitions were latent in his mind; besides, he knew well the stories told by the indian medicine-men in their winter camps,

of the snow-walkers and the spectres, and the formless evil beings that haunt the forest depths, and then dog and waylay the lonely wanderer who after nightfall passes through the regions where they lurk; and it may be that when overcome by the horror of the fate that befell his friend, and when oppressed by the awful dread of the unknown, he grew to attribute, both at the time and still more in remembrance, weird elfin traits to what was merely some wicked and cunning wild beast; but whether this was so or not, no man can say.

When the event occurred, Bauman was still a young man, and was trapping with a partner among the mountains dividing the forks of the salmon from the head of the Wisdom River. Having had not much luck, he and his partner determined to go up into a particularly wild and lonely pass through which ran a small stream said to contain many beavers. The pass had an evil reputation because the year before a solitary hunter who had wandered into it was slain, seemingly by a wild beast, the half eaten remains being afterwards found by some mining prospectors who had passed his camp only the night before.

The memory of this event, however, weighed very lightly with the two trappers, who were as adventurous and hardy as others of their kind. They took their two lean mountain ponies to the foot of the pass where they left them in an open beaver meadow, the rocky timber-clad ground being from there onward impractical for horses. They then struck out on foot through the vast gloomy forest, and in about four hours reached a little open glade where they concluded to camp, as signs of game were plenty.

There was still an hour or two of daylight left, and after building a brush lean-to and throwing down and opening their packs, they started up-stream. The country was very dense and hard to travel through, as there was much down timber, although here and there the sombre woodland was broken by small glades of mountain grass. At dusk they again reached camp. The glade in which it was pitched was not many yards wide, the tall, close-set pines and firs rising round it like a wall. On one side was a little stream, beyond which rose the steep mountain slope, covered with the unbroken growth of evergreen forest.

They were surprised to find that during their absence something, apparently a bear, had visited camp, and had rummaged about among their things, scattering the contents of their packs, and in sheer wantonness destroying their lean-to. The footprints of the beast were quite plain, but at first they paid no particular heed to them, busying themselves with rebuilding the lean-to, laying out their beds and stores and lighting the fire.

While Bauman was making ready supper, it being already dark, his companion began to examine the tracks more closely, and soon took a brand from the fire to follow them up, where the intruder had walked along a game trail after leaving the camp. When the brand flickered out, he returned and took another, repeating his inspection of the footprints very closely. Coming back to the fire, he stood by a minute or two, peering out into the darkness, and suddenly remarked, "Bauman, that bear has been walking on two legs." Bauman laughed at this, but his partner insisted that he was right, and upon again examining the tracks with a torch, they certainly did seem to be made by but two paws or feet. However, it was too dark to make sure. After discussing whether the footprints could possibly be those of a human being, and coming to the conclusion that they could not be, the two men rolled up in their blankets, and went to sleep under the lean-to.

At midnight Bauman was awakened by some noise, and sat up in his blankets. As he did so his nostrils were struck by a strong, wild-beast odor, and he caught the loom of a great body in the darkness at the mouth of the lean-to. Grasping his rifle, he fired at the vague threatening shadow, but must have missed, for immediately afterwards he heard the smashing of the under-wood as the thing, whatever it was, rushed off into the impenetrable blackness of the forest and the night.

After this the men slept but little, sitting up by the rekindled fire, but they heard nothing more. In the morning they started out to look at the few traps they had set the previous evening and put out new ones. By an unspoken agreement they kept together all day, and returned to camp towards evening.

On nearing it they saw, hardly to their astonishment, that the lean-to had again been torn down. The visitor of the preceding day had returned, and in wanton malice had tossed about their camp kit and bedding, and destroyed the shanty. The ground was marked up by its tracks, and on leaving the camp it had gone along the soft earth by the brook. The footprints were as plain as if on snow, and, after a careful scrutineer of the trail, it certainly did seem as if, whatever the thing was, it had walked off on but two legs.

The men, thoroughly uneasy, gathered a great heap of dead logs and kept up a roaring fire throughout the night, one or the other sitting on guard most of the time. About midnight the thing came down through the forest opposite, across the brook, and stayed there on the hillside for nearly an hour. They could hear the branches crackle as it moved about, and several times it uttered a harsh, grating, long-drawn moan, a peculiar sinister sound. Yet it did not venture near the fire.

In the morning the two trappers, after discussing the strange events of the last 36 hours, decided that they should shoulder their packs and leave the valley that afternoon. They were more ready to do this because in spite of seeing good game sign they had caught very little fur. However, it was necessary first to go along the line of their traps and gather them, and this they started out to do. All the morning they kept together, picking up trap after trap, each one empty. On first leaving camp they had the disagreeable sensation of being followed. In the dense spruce thickets they occasionally heard a branch snap after they had passed; and now and then there were slight rustling noises among the small pines to one side of them.

At noon they were back within a couple miles of camp. In the high, bright sunlight their fears seemed absurd to the two armed men, accustomed as they were, through long years of lonely wandering in the wilderness, to face every kind of danger from man, brute, or element. There were still three beaver traps to collect from a little pond in a wide ravine nearby. Bauman volunteered to gather these and bring them in, while his companion went ahead to camp and made ready the packs.

On reaching the pond, Bauman found three beavers in the traps, one of which had been pulled loose and carried into the beaver house. He took several hours securing and preparing the beaver, and when he started homewards he marked, with some uneasiness, how low the sun was getting. As he hurried toward camp, under the tall trees, the silence and desolation of the forest weighted upon him. His feet made no sound on the pine needles and the slanting sunrays, striking through among the straight trunks, made a gray twilight in which objects at a distance glimmered indistinctly. There was nothing to break the gloomy stillness which, when there is no breeze, always broods over these sombre primeval forests.

At last he came to the edge of the little glade where the camp lay and shouted as he approached it, but got no answer. The campfire had gone out, though thin blue smoke was still curling upwards.

Near it lay the packs wrapped and arranged. At first Bauman could see nobody; nor did he receive an answer to his call. Stepping forward he again shouted, and as he did so his eye fell on the body of his friend, stretched beside the trunk of a great fallen spruce. Rushing towards it the horrified trapper found that the body was still warm, but that the neck was broken, while there were four great fang marks at the throat.

The footprints of the unknown beast-creature, printed deep in the soft soil, told the whole story.

The unfortunate man, having finished his packing, had sat down on the spruce log with his face to the fire, and his back to the dense woods, to wait for his companion. While thus waiting, his monstrous assailant, which must have been lurking in the woods, waiting for a chance to catch one of the adventurers unprepared, came silently up from behind, walking with long, noiseless steps and seemingly still on two legs. Evidently unheard, it reached the man, and broke his neck by wrenching his head back with its forepaws, while it buried its teeth in his throat. It had not eaten the body, but apparently had romped and gambolled around it in uncouth, ferocious glee, occasionally rolling over it; it had then fled back into the soundless depth of the woods.

Bauman, utterly unnerved and believing the creature with which he had to deal was something either half-human or half-devil, some great goblin-beast, abandoned everything but his rifle and struck off at speed down the pass, not halting until he reached the beaver meadows where the hobbled ponies were still grazing. Mounting, he rode onwards through the night, until beyond reach of pursuit.

Ape Canyon

One of the most well-documented and sensationalized Sasquatch encounters occurred in 1924, in a remote area of Washington State known as Ape Canyon. Located just northeast of Washington state's Mount St. Helens, Ape Canyon is a narrowing gorge that has become well known for its connection to one of the most renowned Sasquatch encounters in cryptozoological history.

The tale begins on a summer night in July 1924 when a small cabin inhabited by a group of miners was reportedly attacked by a band of wild "apemen." The five miners, who all survived the incident and appeared convinced of its authenticity, were asleep when the assault began.

Suddenly, their hand-built cabin was bombarded with large stones, seemingly thrown by "mountain devils" from all directions. The men retaliated by firing at the creatures, causing the attacks to momentarily cease, only to resume minutes later. At one point, one of the alleged Sasquatch reached into the cabin through a hole in the structure and grabbed an ax but was thwarted before it could extract it from the building.

Photo courtesy of Marc Myrsell.

The onslaught persisted until dawn, at which point the men cautiously emerged from the cabin. One of the miners, Fred Beck, spotted one of the Sasquatch creatures standing at the edge of what is now known as Ape Canyon. Beck shot at the creature, allegedly watching it fall into the gorge.

Beck later authored a book about their harrowing experience titled *I Fought The Ape Men of Mt. St. Helens*. However, more rational theories have also been proposed. The most widely accepted explanation for the sensational tale is that a group of local youths were the ones pelting the cabin with rocks, a common pastime for youngsters. The canyon's acoustics could have distorted their voices, making them sound monstrous.—or even extra-dimensional.

Photo courtesy of Marc Myrsell.

Although some have claimed in recent years to find it, I believe the exact location of the cabin is still unknown. Ape Canyon remains a favored hiking spot, despite being significantly transformed by the eruption of Mount St. Helens in 1980. It appears that neither the threat of otherworldly Sasquatches nor active volcanoes can deter people from visiting this beautiful location.

Marc Myrsell, a land surveyor and renowned Sasquatch historian, has made numerous journeys to the Ape Canyon site. His invaluable assistance has led to the discovery of the original cabin's remains. During a summer expedition in 2023, Braden and Jared Mitchell, descendants of one of the survivors from the incident, rediscovered the entrance to the Vanderwhite mine, a remarkable find. Myrsell, deeply invested in the subject, authored a book titled *"Mountain Devil: The 1924 Ape Canyon Attack and its aftermath,"* which delves into the historical facts surrounding the event. Although the book spans only thirty pages, it is brimming with insightful information.

Over the years, the Ape Canyon Incident has continued to fascinate those who hear it. In its own way furthering the interest in Sasquatch and prompting further investigations. While skeptics dismissed the incident as a hoax or misinterpretation, the consistency of the miners' testimonies and the physical evidence found at the scene, in my opinion, added credibility to their claims.

The Albert Osman Story

In the annals of Sasquatch lore, few stories captivate the imagination quite like the account of Albert Ostman's alleged abduction by a Sasquatch. Ostman's tale, which emerged in the mid-20th century, has been the subject of intense scrutiny and debate.

In 1924, Albert Ostman, a Canadian prospector and outdoorsman, embarked on a solo expedition in the remote Toba Inlet region of British Columbia. While Ostman was camping near a small lake, he claimed to have been forcibly abducted by a family of Sasquatch creatures.

According to Ostman's account, he awoke one night to find himself being carried away by a female Sasquatch. He estimated her height to be around seven to eight feet tall, with long, shaggy hair and a powerful build. Ostman was taken to a nearby valley, where he was held captive for six days by the Sasquatch family.

During his alleged captivity, Ostman claimed to have observed the behavior and habits of the Sasquatch family. He described them as primitive, yet intelligent beings, capable of constructing crude shelters and communicating through a series of grunts and gestures. Ostman also noted they seemed to survive on a diet consisting of mostly of roots, berries, and fish.

Ostman's account detailed his attempts to escape, including a failed effort to overpower the male Sasquatch guarding him. Eventually, he managed to exploit the curiosity of the creatures by offering the big male a sniff from a tin of snuff tobacco. While they were distracted, Ostman made his escape, fleeing back to civilization.

Supporters of Ostman's story point to several factors that they believe lend credibility to his account. Firstly, Ostman maintained his story consistently throughout his life, never wavering in his claims. He also provided detailed descriptions of the Sasquatch family and their behavior, which some argue would be difficult to fabricate.

Interestingly, Ostman's story predates the modern era of Sasquatch fascination, making it less likely that he would have concocted such a tale for personal gain or attention. It is worth noting that Ostman had no apparent motive to perpetuate a hoax, as he did not seek fame or fortune from his encounter.

Skeptics, on the other hand, raise several points that cast doubt on Ostman's story. Many question the lack of physical evidence to support his claims.

Critics also argue that Ostman's account contains inconsistencies and implausible elements. For instance, they question how a lone prospector could have been overpowered and abducted by a family of Sasquatch without sustaining any injuries. Additionally, some find it suspicious that Ostman's story emerged decades after the alleged event, leaving room for embellishment or fabrication.

Despite all this, the Albert Ostman abduction story remains one of the most intriguing and controversial accounts in the realm of Sasquatch encounters. While supporters argue that Ostman's consistent narrative and lack of personal gain lend credibility to his claims, skeptics point to the absence of physical evidence and inconsistencies within his story.

Ultimately, the truth behind Ostman's alleged abduction may never be definitively determined. The account continues to fuel speculation and debate within the Bigfoot research community. Whether it is a remarkable tale of survival or an elaborate hoax, the Ostman story serves as a reminder of the enduring fascination and mystery surrounding the elusive creature known as Sasquatch.

William Roe Sighting

The William Roe Sasquatch sighting, which occurred in October 1955, is one of the most well-documented and intriguing encounters with the elusive creature known as Bigfoot or Sasquatch. This report aims to provide a highly detailed, factual, and comprehensive analysis of the incident, examining the circumstances, witness testimony, physical evidence, and subsequent investigations.

In October 1955, William Roe, a Canadian prospector, was hunting for gold in the remote wilderness near Tete Jaune Cache, British Columbia. While Roe was resting near a creek, he suddenly encountered a large, bipedal creature estimated to be around seven to eight feet tall, covered in dark hair, and possessing human-like features. Roe reported that the creature stood motionless for a few moments before disappearing into the dense forest.

Roe's detailed account of the encounter provides valuable insights into the sighting. According to his testimony, the creature had a conical-shaped head, a prominent brow ridge, deep-set eyes, a flat nose, and a wide mouth. Its arms were long and muscular, reaching below the knees, while its feet were large and covered in hair. Roe estimated the weight of the creature to be around three hundred pounds. He described its hair as dark brown and approximately six inches in length. The most compelling aspect of his encounter for me, is that the creature he saw was female. He describes the exposed breasts, and he would eventually produce a drawing of the creature done by his daughter as he described what he saw. If Sasquatch exists, it should come as no shock that there are females, yet to my knowledge most of the eyewitness accounts appear to be large males. The fact that Roe described seeing a female, is certainly an unusual detail. We would see this same anomaly play out a decade later when Roger Patterson and Bob Gimlin stumble upon what appears to be a very similar specimen on a sand bar in California.

Following the encounter, Roe swore to his account in a written affidavit in front of William Clark, a Commissioner for Oats in and for the Province of Alberta. This is his sworn affidavit.

Ever since I was a small boy back in the forest of Michigan, I have studied the lives and habits of wild animals. Later, when I supported my family in Northern Alberta by hunting and trapping, I spent many hours just observing the wild things. They fascinated me. But the most incredible experience I ever had with a wild creature occurred near a little town called Tete Jaune Cache, British Columbia, about eighty miles west of Jasper, Alberta.

I had been working on the highway near Tete Jaune Cache for about two years. In October 1955, I decided to climb five miles up Mica Mountain to an old deserted mine, just for something to do. I came in sight of the mine about three o'clock in the afternoon after an easy climb. I had just come out of a patch of low brush into a clearing when I saw what I thought was a grizzly bear, in the bush on the other side. I had shot a grizzly near that spot the year before. This one was only about 75 yards away, but I didn't want to shoot it, for I had no way of getting it out. So I sat down on a small rock and watched, my rifle in my hands.

I could see part of the animal's head and the top of one shoulder. A moment later it raised up and stepped out into the opening. Then I saw it was not a bear.

This, to the best of my recollection, is what the creature looked like and how it acted as it came across the clearing directly toward me. My first impression was of a huge man, about six feet tall, almost three feet wide, and probably weighing somewhere near three hundred pounds. It was covered from head to foot with dark brown silver-tipped hair. But as it came closer I saw by its breasts that it was female.

And yet, its torso was not curved like a female's. Its broad frame was straight from shoulder to hip. Its arms were much thicker than a man's arms, and longer, reaching almost to its knees. Its feet were broader proportionately than a man's, about five inches wide at the front and tapering to much thinner heels. When it walked it placed the heel of its foot down first, and I could see the grey-brown skin or hide on the soles of its feet.

It came to the edge of the bush I was hiding in, within twenty feet of me, and squatted down on its haunches. Reaching out its hands it pulled the branches of bushes toward it and stripped the leaves with its teeth. Its lips curled flexibly around the leaves as it ate. I was close enough to see that its teeth were white and even.

The shape of this creature's head somewhat resembled a Negro's. The head was higher at the back than at the front. The nose was broad and flat. The lips and chin protruded farther than its nose. But the hair that covered it, leaving bare only the parts of its face around the mouth, nose and ears, made it resemble an animal as much as a human. None of this hair, even on the back of its head, was longer than an inch, and that on its face was much shorter. Its ears were shaped like a human's ears. But its eyes were small and black like a bear's. And its neck also was unhuman. Thicker and shorter than any man's I had ever seen.

As I watched this creature, I wondered if some movie company was making a film at this place and that what I saw was an actor, made up to look partly human and partly animal. But as I observed it more, I decided it would be impossible to fake such a specimen. Anyway, I learned later there was no such company near that area. Nor, in fact, did anyone live up Mica Mountain, according to the people who lived in Tete Jaune Cache.

Finally, the wild thing must have got my scent, for it looked directly at me through an opening in the brush. A look of amazement crossed its face. It looked so comical at the moment I had to grin. Still in a crouched position, it backed up three or four short steps, then straightened up to its full height and started to walk rapidly back the way it had come. For a moment it watched me over its shoulder as it went, not exactly afraid, but as though it wanted no contact with anything strange.

The thought came to me that if I shot it, I would possibly have a specimen of great interest to scientists the world over. I had heard stories of the Sasquatch, the giant hairy Indians that live in the legends of British Columbia Indians, and also many claim, are still in fact alive today. Maybe this was a Sasquatch, I told myself.

I leveled my rifle. The creature was still walking rapidly away, again turning its head to look in my direction. I lowered the rifle. Although I have called the creature "it", I felt now that it was a human being and I knew I would never forgive myself if I killed it.

Just as it came to the other patch of brush it threw its head back and made a peculiar noise that seemed to be half laugh and half language, and which I can only describe as a kind of a whinny. Then it walked from the small brush into a stand of lodgepole pine.

I stepped out into the opening and looked across a small ridge just beyond the pine to see if I could see it again. It came out on the ridge a couple of hundred yards away from me, tipped its head back again, and again emitted the only sound I had heard it make, but what this half- laugh, half-language was meant to convey, I do not know. It disappeared then, and I never saw it again.

I wanted to find out if it lived on vegetation entirely or ate meat as well, so I went down and looked for signs. I found it in five different places, and although I examined it thoroughly, could find no hair or shells of bugs or insects. So I believe it was strictly a vegetarian.

I found one place where it had slept for a couple of nights under a tree. Now, the nights were cool up the mountain, at this time of year especially, and yet it had not used a fire. I found no sign that it possessed even the simplest of tools. Nor a single companion while in this place.

Whether this was a Sasquatch I do not know. It will always remain a mystery to me, unless another one is found.

I hereby declare the above statement to be in every part true, to the best of my powers of observation and recollection."

(Signed) William Roe

The William Roe Sasquatch sighting remains one of the most compelling and well-documented encounters with the elusive creature. His encounter provides valuable insight that continues to fuel the ongoing debate surrounding the existence of this mysterious creature.

The Ruby Creek Incident

The Ruby Creek Bigfoot Incident was reported in 1941 near Ruby Creek, British Columbia, Canada. The incident involved a local family, the Chapmans, who claimed to have encountered the creature.

According to the family's account, Jeannie Chapman and her children first noticed a large, hairy creature approaching their home while her husband, George, was away. Initially mistaking it for a bear, they soon realized it was something else due to its immense size and human-like features. The creature was described as standing about ten feet tall, covered in long hair, and having a distinctly human-like form.

Upon returning home, George found large footprints around their property. The creature had reportedly also interacted with a 55-gallon barrel of salted fish, which was found tossed aside.

The story spread, contributing to the Sasquatch legend.

Ivan T Sanderson wrote about the encounter in *True Magazine* in 1960.

Stories about the Sasquatch have been appearing in print from time to time since the 1860s, and I have clipping in my files from almost every year since the early 1920s. But the modern history of the Sasquatch really dates from September 1941, when one of these creatures paid a visit — in broad daylight — to an Indian family named Chapman. While the Amerindian stories have usually been dismissed as legend, or laughed off because Indians are not supposed to be reliable, this experience was accompanied by too much physical evidence to be ignored.

The Chapman family consisted off George and Jeannie Chapman and children numbering, at my visit, four. Mr. Chapman worked on the railroad, and was living at that time in a small place called Ruby Creek, 30 miles up the Fraser River from Agassiv, British Columbia, in Canada's great western province.

It was about 3 in the afternoon of a sunny, cloudless day when Jeannie Chapman's eldest son, then aged 9, came running to the house saying that there was a cow coming down out of the woods at the foot of the nearby mountain. The other kids, a boy aged 7 and a little girl of 5, were still playing in a field behind the house bordering on the rail track.

Mrs. Chapman went out to look, since the boy seemed oddly disturbed, and they saw what at first she thought was a very big bear moving about among the bushes bordering the field beyond the railway tracks. She called the two children who came running immediately. Then the creature moved onto the tracks and she saw to her horror that it was a gigantic man covered with hair, not fur. The hair seemed to be about four inches long all over, and of a pale yellow-brown color. To pin down this color Mrs. Chapman pointed out to me a sheet of lightly varnished plywood in the room where we were sitting. This was of a brown-ochre color.

This creature advanced directly toward the house and Mrs. Chapman had, as she put it, "much too much time to look at it" because she stood her ground outside while the eldest boy — on her instructions — got a blanket from the house and rounded up the other children. The kids were in a near panic, she told us, and it took two or three minutes to get the blanket, during which time the creature had reached the near corner of the field only about 100 feet away from her. Mrs. Chapman then spread the blanket and, holding it aloft so that the kids could not see the creature or it them, she backed off at the double to the old field and down on to the river beach out of sight, and then ran with the kids downstream to the village.

I asked her a leading question about the blanket. Had her purpose in using it been to prevent her kids seeing the creature, in accord with an alleged Amerindian belief that to do so brings bad luck and often death? Her reply was both prompt and surprising. She said that, although she had heard white men tell of that belief, she had not heard it from her parents or any other of her people whose advice regarding the so-called Sasquatch had been simply not to go further than certain points up certain valleys, to run if she saw one, and not to struggle if one caught her as it might squeeze her to death by mistake.

'No,' she said, 'I used the blanket because I thought it was after one of the kids and so might go into the house to look for them instead of following me.' This seems to have been sound logic as the creature did go into the house and also rummaged through an old outhouse pretty thoroughly, hauling from it a 55-gallon barrel of salt fish, breaking this open, and scattering its contents about outside. (The irony of it is that all those three children DID die within three years; the two boys by drowning, and the little girl on a sickbed. And just after I interviewed the Chapmans they also were drowned in the Fraser River when a row-boat capsized.)

Mrs. Chapman told me that the creature was about 7½ feet tall. She could estimate its height by the various fence and line posts standing about the field. It had a rather small head and a very short, thick neck; in fact really no neck at all, a point that was emphasized by William Roe and by all others who claim to have seen one of these creatures. Its body was entirely human in shape except that it was immensely thick through its chest and its arms were exceptionally long. She did not see the feet which were in the grass. Its shoulders were very wide and it had no breasts, from which Mrs. Chapman assumed it was a male, though she also did not see any male genitalia due to the long hair covering its groin. She was most definite on one point: the naked parts of its face and its hands were much darker than its hair, and appeared to be almost black.

George Chapman returned home from his work on the railroad that day shortly before 6 in the evening and by a route that by-passed the village so that he saw no one to tell him what had happened. When he reached his house he immediately saw the woodshed door battered in, and spotted enormous humanoid footprints all over the place. Greatly alarmed — for he, like all of his people, had heard since childhood about the "big wild men of the mountains," though he did not hear the word Sasquatch till after this incident — he called for his family and then dashed through the house. Then he spotted the foot-tracks of his wife and kids going off toward the river. He followed these until he picked them up on the sand beside the river and saw them going off downstream without any giant ones following.

Somewhat relieved, he was retracing his steps when he stumbled across the giant's foot-tracks on the river bank farther upstream. These had come down out of the potato patch, which lay between the house and the river, had milled about by the river, and then gone back through the old field toward the foot of the mountains where they disappeared in the heavy growth.

Returning to the house, relieved to know that the tracks of all four of his family had gone off downstream to the village, George Chapman went to examine the woodshed. In our interview, after 18 years, he still expressed voluble astonishment that any living thing, even a 7-foot-6- inch man with a barrel-chest could lift a 55-gallon tub of fish and break it open without using a tool. He confirmed the creature's height after finding a number of long brown hairs stuck in the slab-wood lintel of the doorway, above the level of his head.

George Chapman then went off to the village to look for his family, and found them in a state of calm collapse. He gathered them up and invited his father-in-law and two others to return with him, for protection of his family when he was away at work.

The foot-tracks returned every night for a week and on two occasions the dogs that the Chapmans had taken with them set up the most awful racket at exactly 2 o'clock in the morning. The Sasquatch did not, however, molest them or, apparently, touch either the house or the woodshed. But the whole business was too unnerving and the family finally moved out. They never went back.

After a long chat about this and other matters, Mrs. Chapman suddenly told us something very significant just as we were leaving. She said: "It made an awful funny noise." I asked her if she could imitate this noise for me but it was her husband who did so, saying that he had heard it at night twice during the week after the first incident. He then proceeded to utter exactly the same strange, gurgling whistle that the men in California, who said they had heard a Bigfoot call, had given us. This is a sound I cannot reproduce in print, but I can assure you that it is unlike anything I have ever heard given by man or beast anywhere in the world.

To me, this information is of the greatest significance. That an Amerindian couple in British Columbia should give out with exactly the same strange sound in connection with a Sasquatch that two highly educated white men did, over 600 miles south in connection with California's Bigfoot, is incredible. If this is all hoax or a publicity stunt, or mass-hallucination, as some people have claimed, how does it happen that this noise — which defies description — always sounds the same no matter who has tried to reproduce it for me?

These were probably the last words on the Sasquatch that the Chapmans uttered and I absolutely refuse to listen to anybody who might say they were lying. Admittedly, honest men are such a rarity as possibly to be non-existent, but I have met a few who could qualify and I put the Chapmans near the head of the list.

While skeptics may dismiss these accounts as mere folklore or exaggerations, the consistency of the descriptions and the impact they had on the explorers' beliefs cannot be easily dismissed. These encounters serve as a testament to the enduring mystery of Sasquatch and its place in the cultural fabric of North America, leaving a legacy that continues to captivate and intrigue researchers and enthusiasts to this day.

In recent decades, advancements in technology and increased public interest have led to a surge in reported Sasquatch sightings. Numerous eyewitness accounts, often accompanied by photographs, videos, or audio recordings, have emerged from various regions across North America.

Investigations by citizen scientists have also played a crucial role in Sasquatch research. Organizations such as the Bigfoot Field Researchers Organization (BFRO) and independent researchers have conducted extensive fieldwork, collecting physical evidence, analyzing footprints, and documenting witness testimonies. While definitive proof of Sasquatch's existence remains elusive, these efforts have contributed to a growing body of knowledge and a deeper understanding of the phenomenon.

The historical record of Sasquatch sightings is a complex tapestry woven with indigenous legends, early explorer accounts, and modern-day eyewitness testimonies. From ancient folklore to contemporary encounters, the presence of Sasquatch has left an indelible mark on human history. While skeptics continue to question the validity of these accounts, the weight of evidence and the consistency of eyewitness testimonies cannot be easily dismissed. The quest for answers continues, as researchers and enthusiasts alike strive to unravel the mystery.

4

BIGFOOT IN POP CULTURE: A PHENOMENON UNLEASHED

We have established that Sasquatch is alive and well in the stories from our past. Its alias, Bigfoot, has also become a present-day iconic figure in popular culture, captivating the imaginations of people worldwide. Over the past five decades, Sasquatch has made numerous appearances in television, film, and various forms of popular media. Let's explore the evolution of Bigfoot in pop culture, highlighting its impact and the references that have solidified its status as a cultural phenomenon.

I often start off interviews with guests on the show who are there to share their Sasquatch encounter stories, "What got you interested in the subject?" The question serves a dual purpose, in that I am genuinely interested in the answer, and their answer often sheds light on their general approach to the phenomenon. That said, more often than not the answers for most involve seeing the Patterson-Gimlin film, at some point, and Sasquatch stories on television.

Many attribute the interest in the subject of Sasquatch to the show *In Search of...* with Leonard Nimoy. That series aired weekly; from 1977 to 1982, focusing on various mysterious phenomena. The show was developed following the success of three one-hour TV documentaries by Alan Landsburg: *In Search of Ancient Astronauts* in 1973, which was based on Erich von Däniken's book *Chariots of the Gods? In Search of Ancient Mysteries* and *The Outer Space Connection,* both in 1975. These documentaries, later adapted into popular paperbacks by Landsburg, featured narration by Rod Serling, who was initially chosen to host the spin-off series. However, Serling passed away before production began, and Leonard Nimoy was chosen as the host. The series was rebooted in 2002 with host Mitch Pileggi and again in 2018 with Zachary Quinto. It is currently being broadcast on the History Channel.

The program delved into investigations surrounding contentious and paranormal phenomena, such as UFOs, Sasquatch, and the Loch Ness Monster. It also showcased episodes revolving around enigmatic historical events and figures, including Anna Anderson/Grand Duchess Anastasia, the Lincoln Assassination, and the Jack the Ripper murders. Also featured were notorious cults like Jim Jones; as well as missing individuals, ships, and cities, such as Amelia Earhart, Jimmy Hoffa, D.B. Cooper, the *Mary Celeste,* the *Titanic,* and the lost Roanoke Colony. Given the show's tendency to explore unconventional subjects and contentious theories, a verbal disclaimer was included in the opening credits of each episode, emphasizing the speculative nature of the evidence and theories presented. In 1978, Landsburg produced a Sasquatch documentary using portions of two *In Search of* episodes ("The Monster Hunters" and "The Yeti") called *Manbeast! Myth or Monster,* based on his book *In Search of Myths and Monsters.* Though Nimoy had written the foreword to Landsburg's book, he did not narrate this documentary.

Just prior to the creation of *In Search Of* one of the earliest television appearances of Sasquatch occurred in the popular series *The Six Million Dollar Man.* In a two-part episode titled "The Secret of Bigfoot," that originally aired February 1, 1976, the bionic hero Steve Austin encounters a towering, hairy creature in the wilderness. This portrayal of Sasquatch as a formidable adversary introduced the creature to a wide audience and sparked interest in its mythology.

In this two-part episode, Steve Austin and Oscar Goldman are part of a team working on advanced earthquake sensors. Two geologists from their team, Ivan and Marlene Bekey, mysteriously disappear. In the vicinity, they find footprints of the legendary creature, Bigfoot. Ivan is found safe but in shock, while Marlene is still missing.

When Bigfoot attacks their base camp, Steve confronts and fights the creature, unaware that aliens from a nearby mountain are watching him. During the fight, one of Bigfoot's arms detaches, revealing it to be a robot, not a real creature. Bigfoot flees, with Steve hot on its trail, leading him to a cave that opens into the mountain where the aliens reside. Steve is swiftly knocked unconscious, captured, and examined by the aliens.

When Steve wakes up, an alien woman named Shalon informs him that the aliens built and controlled Bigfoot for their protection. The earthquake sensor team was targeted because they had found a volcanic vent that powered the alien colony. Meanwhile, Oscar learns that a major earthquake is imminent along the main San Medrian fault line, threatening all the cities on the California west coast. The only solution is to trigger a controlled underground nuclear explosion to create a smaller, man-made earthquake along a minor tributary fault line, which would prevent the main earthquake. Oscar gives the green light, fully aware that Steve and the still-missing Marlene are in serious danger from the explosion and the subsequent earthquake.

The American fantasy comedy film *Harry and the Hendersons* released in June 1987 brought Bigfoot into the realm of family-friendly entertainment. The story revolves around a suburban family who accidentally hits a Sasquatch-like creature with their car and decides to take it home. The film portrays Bigfoot, named Harry, as a gentle and lovable creature, challenging the traditional perception of Bigfoot as a menacing figure. *Harry and the Hendersons* became a box-office success and further popularized the image of Sasquatch as a friendly and misunderstood creature.

Harry and the Hendersons was directed and produced by William Dear, featuring a star-studded cast including John Lithgow, Melinda Dillon, Don Ameche, David Suchet, Margaret Langrick, Joshua Rudoy, Lainie Kazan, and Kevin Peter Hall. Steven Spielberg was the uncredited executive producer, while Rick Baker was responsible for the makeup and creature designs for the character Harry.

The film narrates the story of a family from Seattle who encounters the mythical creature Sasquatch, drawing inspiration from the numerous reported sightings in the Pacific Northwest, California, and other parts of the United States and Canada over three centuries. The film was shot in various locations in the Cascade Range of Washington state near Interstate 90 and the town of Index near US 2, as well as in Seattle's Wallingford, Ballard, and Beacon Hill neighborhoods and other locations in or around Seattle.

Harry and the Hendersons was a commercial success, grossing $50 million worldwide. It was awarded an Oscar for Best Makeup at the 60th Academy Awards and even inspired a television spin-off of the same name. In the United Kingdom, the film was initially released as *Bigfoot and the Hendersons*, but the television series kept the American title. The DVD and all current showings of the film in the UK now use the original title.

Finding Bigfoot, the popular television show that aired on Animal Planet from 2011 to 2018, had a profound impact on Sasquatch research and brought the subject of the existence of Sasquatch into millions of homes worldwide. The show followed four researchers -- James "Bobo" Fay, Cliff Barackman, Matt Moneymaker, and Ranae Holland - as they traveled across North America, investigating reported sightings of the legendary creature.

The show's cast was a diverse group, each bringing a unique perspective to the research. James "Bobo" Fay, a commercial fisherman and

Sasquatch enthusiast, was known for his deep belief in the creature's existence. Cliff Barackman, a former science teacher, brought a scientific approach to the investigations, often providing logical explanations for the phenomena they encountered. Matt Moneymaker, the founder of the Bigfoot Field Researchers Organization (BFRO), was the driving force behind the team's investigations, while Ranae Holland, a field biologist, served as the team's skeptic, always questioning the evidence, and pushing for more concrete proof.

Finding Bigfoot played a significant role in popularizing Sasquatch research. The show's format, which involved interviewing witnesses, conducting night investigations, and analyzing evidence, provided viewers with an inside look at how Sasquatch research is conducted. It also helped to dispel some of the myths and misconceptions about Sasquatch, presenting the creature as a possible undiscovered primate rather than a supernatural entity.

I truly believe that the show helped to bring the subject of Sasquatch into mainstream conversation. By presenting the investigations in an entertaining and accessible format, the show reached a wide audience, sparking interest and curiosity about the creature. Its popularity led to an increase in reported Sasquatch sightings and inspired many viewers to conduct their own investigations.

Despite its entertainment value, *Finding Bigfoot* also contributed to the scientific study of the creature. The cast's rigorous approach to investigations, their use of modern technology, and their commitment to analyzing all evidence critically added a level of credibility to the field. The show also highlighted the importance of eyewitness accounts, which are often dismissed in mainstream science but are a crucial component of Sasquatch research. Though the series ended in 2018, its impact is indisputable. The celebrities from the well-liked show continue to make appearances at numerous events and conferences across the United States to this day.

Sasquatch has also made appearances in various forms of pop culture media beyond television and film. It has been referenced in cartoons like *The Simpsons*, where the character Homer Simpson encounters a Bigfoot-like creature in the episode "Treehouse of Horror VI" (1995). Bigfoot has also been featured in video games, such as *Grand Theft Auto: San Andreas* (2004), where players can encounter a Bigfoot-like creature in the wilderness.

Sasquatch has become a staple in advertising and marketing campaigns. It has been used to promote products ranging from outdoor gear to beverages, capitalizing on its iconic status and the intrigue it generates.

- Jack Link's Beef Jerky has a popular commercial series called "Messin' with Sasquatch" wherein hikers prank Sasquatch, leading to humorous retaliations from the creature.
- Bushnell Corporation, a game camera manufacturer, and *Field & Stream* launched a contest in 2007 over a photo taken by deer hunter Rick Jacobs, which some believe could be a young Sasquatch. The companies offered a one-million-dollar reward for a verifiable Sasquatch photo taken on a game camera.
- Red Robin, a food chain, aired a TV commercial where a hiker says, "Red Robin" and gets a "Yummm" response from Bigfoot.
- Boston Pizza used a Bigfoot character named "Louie" in their TV commercials in 2007, but later decided to discontinue the character.
- Kokanee Beer featured a Bigfoot named "Mel" in their commercials, who was pitted against the "Kokanee Ranger" played by John Novak. In 2004, a statue of Mel was erected in Creston, British Columbia, with half the construction costs covered by the Columbia Brewery Company.
- Carlsberg Beer used a Bigfoot suit in two of their commercials, which were not well-received.
- American Comfort technology company, Purple, launched a YouTube ad in November 2016 titled, "Can Your Mattress

Protector Stand up to Sasquatch?". The ad humorously features a Bigfoot family and has garnered over 128 million views as of January 2022.

- Progressive, an American insurance company, aired a commercial in March 2020 featuring a Bigfoot named "Darryl" conversing with fictional saleswoman Flo.
- Dr. Squatch, a personal care products company, uses a parody of the name "Sasquatch" in their brand and logo.
- Sierra Nevada Brewing Company brews a barley wine-style ale named "Bigfoot".
- The U.S. Forest Service uses Bigfoot in humorous environmental protection campaigns.
- In 2020, Oregon's fire safety officials launched a forest fire safety campaign called "Safer with Sasquatch."
- Chuck E. Cheese's has a Bigfoot character named Nigel.
- During the COVID-19 pandemic, Sasquatch was used as a symbol for various social distancing campaigns.

Sasquatch's presence in pop culture has evolved over the past five decades, solidifying its status as a cultural phenomenon. From its early appearances in television shows like *The Six Million Dollar Man* to its portrayal as a lovable creature in *Harry and the Hendersons*, Sasquatch has captured the imagination of audiences worldwide.

As Sasquatch continues to captivate the public's imagination, its presence in pop culture serves as a reminder of the enduring allure of the unknown and the fascination with phenomena that exist on the fringes of our understanding. Whether as a menacing adversary or a misunderstood creature, Bigfoot's place in popular culture is firmly established, leaving an indelible mark on the collective consciousness of society.

Sasquatch's Popularity: A Catalyst for Increased Sighting Reports?

As we just discussed, Sasquatch's popularity in pop culture has soared over the years with countless books, movies, and television shows dedicated to the elusive creature. This raises the intriguing question of whether Sasquatch's presence in pop culture could contribute to an increase in sighting reports. By examining the potential effects of media exposure and cultural influence, we can gain insights into the complex relationship between the creatures' popularity and the frequency of reported sightings.

The Power of Suggestion

One argument suggests that Sasquatch's popularity in pop culture could influence individuals to interpret their encounters as Sasquatch sightings. When people are exposed to images, stories, and depictions of Sasquatch through various media, it may create a cognitive bias, leading them to perceive ambiguous or unexplained phenomena as evidence of Sasquatch's existence.

This phenomenon, known as the "power of suggestion," can shape people's discernment and contribute to an increase in reported sightings. The power of suggestion is a potent psychological tool that can shape our perceptions, beliefs, and actions. It is a force that can subtly manipulate our minds, often without our conscious awareness. This psychological phenomenon can certainly play a role in the experiences of individuals who claim to have encountered a Sasquatch.

The power of suggestion operates on the principle that our minds are susceptible to ideas or thoughts, which can influence our perceptions of reality. This susceptibility is heightened when we are in a state of heightened emotion or stress, conditions often reported during alleged Sasquatch encounters.

When an individual claims to have encountered Sasquatch, it is essential to consider the context in which the encounter occurred. Often, these encounters happen in remote wooded areas typically associated with Sasquatch sightings. The individual may already be aware of the Sasquatch legend and may have pre-existing expectations or fears. This setting, combined with the individual's heightened emotional state, creates a fertile ground for the power of suggestion to take root.

The power of suggestion can manifest in several ways in these encounters. For instance, an individual might misinterpret natural sounds or sights as evidence of Sasquatch. A rustling in the bushes could be perceived as the movement of the creature, or a shadow cast by the moonlight might be interpreted as the silhouette of the elusive beast. The individual's mind, influenced by the power of suggestion, fills in the gaps, transforming ambiguous stimuli into a perceived encounter with Sasquatch.

The power of suggestion can also influence individuals after the encounter. When sharing their experiences, individuals may unconsciously embellish or modify their stories due to the reactions or suggestions of others. For example, if a listener expresses skepticism unless the individual sees the creature's distinctive footprints, the individual might "remember" seeing such footprints, even if they did not initially recall such a detail. This phenomenon, known as "memory conformity," demonstrates how suggestibility can shape our recollections.

The power of suggestion can also play a role in group encounters with Sasquatch. In these situations, one person's interpretation of an event can influence how others perceive it. This is known as "social contagion," a form of mass suggestion where one person's panic or misinterpretation can spread through a group, leading everyone to believe they've encountered Sasquatch.

However, acknowledging the power of suggestion does not necessarily discredit all Sasquatch encounters. It merely provides a psychological explanation for some experiences. It is crucial to approach each claim with an open mind, balancing healthy skepticism with respect for the individual's experience.

The power of suggestion is a significant factor to consider when examining claims of Sasquatch encounters. It can shape perceptions, influence memories, and even spread through groups, creating shared experiences based on suggestion rather than objective reality. Understanding this power can help us navigate the fascinating, often murky waters of Sasquatch encounters, providing a lens through which we can view these experiences with both empathy and critical analysis.

The Availability Heuristic

The availability heuristic is another psychological concept that may contribute to an increase in Sasquatch sighting reports. This heuristic (or bias) refers to the tendency of individuals to rely on readily available information when making judgments or decisions. When Sasquatch is prominently featured in pop culture, it becomes more accessible in people's minds. As a result, when individuals encounter something unusual or unexplained in the wilderness, their minds may automatically associate it with Sasquatch due to its availability in their mental framework.

The availability heuristic is a mental shortcut that relies on immediate examples that come to mind when evaluating a specific topic, concept, method, or decision. It operates on the notion that if something can be recalled, it must be important, or at least more important than alternative solutions which are not as readily recalled. This can have profound effects on individuals who research or claim to have encountered a Sasquatch.

The availability heuristic can significantly shape the perceptions and beliefs of individuals. When a researcher is exposed to a multitude of accounts, stories, and alleged evidence of Sasquatch's existence, these readily available pieces of information can sway their judgment. The more frequently they encounter such information, the more likely they are to believe in Sasquatch's existence, regardless of the scientific validity or credibility of the sources. This is because the availability heuristic makes it easier for them to recall these instances, thus making them seem more prevalent and credible.

For instance, a researcher might come across numerous footprint casts purportedly belonging to Sasquatch. The sheer volume of these casts, coupled with the vivid descriptions and passionate assertions of those who found them, can make the evidence seem compelling. The availability heuristic kicks in, making these examples readily accessible in the researcher's mind, thereby influencing their belief in the creature's existence.

Similarly, individuals who claim to have encountered Sasquatch are also influenced by the availability heuristic. Their personal experience, being highly vivid and emotionally charged, is easily recalled. This makes it seem more significant than other pieces of information, such as the lack of definitive scientific evidence supporting Sasquatch's existence. The encounter, being readily available in their memory, influences their belief and perception, making them more likely to assert the existence of Sasquatch.

The availability heuristic can also lead to a confirmation bias among Sasquatch researchers and witnesses. Once they believe in Sasquatch's existence, they are more likely to notice and remember information that confirms their belief, while ignoring or forgetting information that contradicts it. This is because confirming information is more readily available to them due to their existing belief.

However, it's crucial to note that the availability heuristic, while influential, does not necessarily lead to accurate beliefs or conclusions. The frequency of information recall does not equate to its truthfulness or validity. Therefore, researchers and individuals who have encountered Sasquatch must strive to critically evaluate the available information, considering its source, credibility, and scientific validity, rather than relying solely on its availability.

The availability heuristic certainly plays a significant role in shaping the beliefs and perceptions of individuals researching or encountering Sasquatch. It influences what information they recall, how they interpret it, and ultimately, what they believe. However, it's essential to be aware of this cognitive bias and strive for a more balanced, critical approach to information evaluation to ensure accurate and reliable conclusions.

Cognitive Dissonance and the Sasquatch Phenomenon

Cognitive dissonance, a psychological theory developed by Leon Festinger in 1957, refers to the mental discomfort experienced by an individual who holds two or more contradictory beliefs, values, or perceptions simultaneously. It is worth exploring how this psychological phenomenon influences both researchers and those who claim to have encountered the elusive creature.

Despite the lack of empirical evidence supporting its existence, a significant number of people claim to have seen or interacted with this creature. This dichotomy between belief and empirical evidence is where cognitive dissonance comes into play.

For Sasquatch researchers, cognitive dissonance can manifest in several ways. Many researchers have dedicated years, even decades, to the pursuit of Sasquatch, investing significant time, energy, and resources. The lack of concrete evidence, however, contradicts their deeply held belief in the creature's existence. This contradiction creates a state of cognitive dissonance, which can be resolved in several ways.

One common method of resolution is to dismiss or downplay the lack of evidence. Researchers may argue that Sasquatch is an exceptionally elusive creature, or that current scientific methods are insufficient to detect it. Another method is to reinterpret the evidence. For example, ambiguous findings such as unidentified hair or footprints might be interpreted as definitive proof of Sasquatch's existence.

For individuals who claim to have encountered Sasquatch, cognitive dissonance can be even more pronounced. These individuals have a direct, personal experience that contradicts the widely accepted scientific consensus. To resolve this dissonance, they may reject the consensus, arguing that science is fallible or that there is a conspiracy to suppress the truth about Sasquatch. Alternatively, they may reinterpret their experience, convincing themselves that they saw a bear or other known animal, rather than a Sasquatch.

Cognitive dissonance can also influence the way these individuals interact with others. They may seek out like-minded individuals or communities, such as online Sasquatch forums, to validate their beliefs and experiences. This can create an echo chamber effect, reinforcing their beliefs and further entrenching them in their cognitive dissonance.

Cognitive dissonance certainly plays a role in the world of Sasquatch research. It influences how researchers interpret evidence, how individuals reconcile their personal experiences with scientific consensus, and how these individuals interact with others. Understanding this psychological phenomenon can provide valuable insights into the human mind and its capacity for belief in the face of contradiction.

Social Contagion

The influence of social contagion on Sasquatch research cannot be overlooked. Social contagion refers to the spread of ideas, emotions, or behaviors within a group through imitation, conformity, or suggestion. By delving into the mechanisms of social contagion, examining case studies, and analyzing the psychological aspects involved, we can gain a deeper understanding of how this phenomenon shapes the Bigfoot research community and eyewitness accounts. The phenomenon of social contagion suggests that the popularity of Sasquatch in pop culture can create a sense of social validation for those who claim to have had sightings.

When Sasquatch sightings gain media attention and become part of public discourse, individuals who have had similar experiences may feel more comfortable coming forward and sharing their stories. This can create a ripple effect, leading to an increase in reported sightings as people seek validation and connection with others who have had similar encounters. Social contagion encompasses various psychological processes that contribute to the transmission of beliefs, behaviors, and experiences within a social group. These mechanisms include conformity, suggestion, and imitation, which can significantly impact the perception and interpretation of Sasquatch encounters.

Within the Sasquatch research community, social contagion can contribute to the formation of shared belief systems. Researchers, driven by a common interest, often engage in discussions, conferences, and online forums, where ideas and experiences are exchanged. This collective sharing can reinforce existing beliefs, intensify confirmation bias, and create a sense of validation among researchers. Social contagion can also lead to group polarization, where researchers become more extreme in their beliefs and interpretations over time. As individuals within the community reinforce each other's ideas, skepticism may diminish, and the acceptance of anecdotal evidence may increase, potentially hindering objective analysis.

Media plays a crucial role in disseminating information about Sasquatch encounters. Sensationalized stories, documentaries, and reality TV shows can influence individuals' perceptions and expectations, leading to an increased likelihood of misinterpretation or fabrication of encounters. Eyewitnesses who claim to have encountered Sasquatch may be susceptible to social contagion effects. When exposed to other accounts, either through personal interactions or media, individuals may unconsciously incorporate elements from these stories into their own experiences, leading to the amplification of details or the creation of false memories.

Social contagion can prime individuals to expect certain experiences during Sasquatch encounters. This expectation bias can influence perception, leading to the misinterpretation of ambiguous stimuli as Sasquatch-related, such as misidentifying common animals or natural phenomena. Emotional contagion, the transmission of emotions within a group, can also impact Sasquatch researchers and eyewitnesses. The excitement, fear, or fascination surrounding Sasquatch encounters can be contagious, intensifying emotional responses and potentially distorting the recall of events.

Social contagion exerts a profound influence on Sasquatch researchers and individuals who claim to have encountered the creature. By understanding the mechanisms of social contagion, recognizing its impact on belief systems, and acknowledging the psychological factors at play, we can approach Sasquatch research and eyewitness accounts with a more critical and discerning perspective. This chapter serves as a comprehensive exploration of the complex interplay between social contagion and the world of Sasquatch research, shedding light on the challenges faced by both researchers and eyewitnesses alike.

Increased Awareness and Reporting Channels

Sasquatch's popularity in pop culture has also led to increased awareness of the creature and the availability of reporting channels. With the rise of the internet and social media, individuals now have platforms to share their experiences and connect with others who have encountered Sasquatch. This ease of communication and the ability to share sightings instantly can contribute to a higher number of reported sightings, as people are more likely to come forward and share their encounters.

In recent years, the field of Sasquatch research has witnessed a surge in public interest and a growing number of reported sightings and encounters. Increased awareness about Sasquatch and the research surrounding it has led to a shift in public perception. What was once dismissed as mere folklore or myth is now being taken more seriously by a broader audience.

The growing acceptance of Sasquatch as a legitimate subject of study has encouraged more individuals to come forward with their encounters, fostering a sense of community among researchers and eyewitnesses.

With more resources available, researchers can invest in advanced equipment, conduct comprehensive field studies, and collaborate with experts from various scientific disciplines, thereby enhancing the credibility and scientific rigor of Sasquatch research. The establishment of reliable reporting channels, such as dedicated websites, hotlines, and research organizations, has provided a platform for eyewitnesses to share their experiences without fear of ridicule or skepticism. By offering a safe and non-judgmental space, these reporting channels encourage individuals to come forward, contributing to a larger database of Sasquatch encounters and enabling researchers to analyze patterns and gather valuable data.

The surge in awareness has attracted researchers from diverse scientific backgrounds, including anthropology, primatology, zoology, and forensic sciences, to collaborate on Sasquatch research.

This interdisciplinary approach allows for a comprehensive analysis of evidence, incorporating methodologies and expertise from various fields, ultimately advancing our understanding of Sasquatch behavior, habitat, and potential existence. Increased awareness has spurred the development of cutting-edge technologies, such as high-resolution cameras, drones, thermal imaging, and DNA analysis techniques, which aid in the collection of more reliable evidence. These technological advancements not only enhance the quality of data but also provide researchers with new tools to investigate Sasquatch sightings and gather tangible evidence, further legitimizing the field of study.

The impact of increased awareness and reporting channels on Sasquatch researchers and eyewitnesses cannot be overstated. By fostering a sense of community, encouraging eyewitnesses to come forward, providing psychological support, and promoting scientific advancements, heightened awareness has propelled Sasquatch research into a new era of credibility and scientific rigor. As we continue to explore this fascinating subject, it is crucial to maintain an open mind, respect the experiences of eyewitnesses, and embrace the potential discoveries that lie ahead.

Podcasts: Fueling the Fire of Sightings

In recent years, the popularity of Sasquatch encounter podcasts, such as my own *Sasquatch Odyssey*, has surged, captivating audiences with tales of mysterious encounters and unexplained phenomena.

Sasquatch encounter podcasts have played a significant role in increasing awareness of the creature and the possibility of encountering Sasquatch. As these podcasts gain popularity and reach wider audiences, they introduce the concept of Sasquatch to individuals who may not have been familiar with it before. Listeners become more aware of the phenomenon and may be more likely to report their own encounters or share stories they have heard from others.

Podcasts provide a convenient and accessible platform for researchers, enthusiasts, and eyewitnesses to share their knowledge, theories, and encounters with a global audience. Unlike traditional media, podcasts are not limited by geographical boundaries, allowing individuals from all corners of the world to engage with Sasquatch research and contribute to the ongoing discourse. Podcasts have played a pivotal role in building a sense of community among Sasquatch researchers, enthusiasts, and witnesses. By featuring interviews, discussions, and listener stories, podcasts create a space for individuals to connect, share their experiences, and find support within a community that understands and validates their encounters.

Podcasts offer witnesses the option to share their encounters anonymously, providing a safe space for individuals who may fear judgment or ridicule. By protecting their identities, witnesses can openly discuss their experiences without the fear of personal repercussions, encouraging more individuals to come forward and contribute to the growing body of Sasquatch encounters. Podcasts provide witnesses with a platform to share their stories and receive validation from hosts, and fellow listeners who have had similar experiences. This validation and support can be instrumental in helping witnesses process their encounters, overcome any emotional distress, and find a sense of belonging within the Sasquatch research community.

Podcasts facilitate collaboration among researchers, allowing them to share their findings, theories, and methodologies with a wider audience. Through interviews and discussions, researchers can exchange ideas, challenge existing beliefs, and collectively work towards advancing our understanding of Sasquatch behavior, habitat, and potential existence. Podcasts also serve as a valuable platform for researchers to disseminate their findings, theories, and research papers to a broader audience. By presenting their work in an accessible and engaging format, researchers can bridge the gap between academia and the general public, fostering a greater appreciation for Sasquatch research and encouraging further exploration.

Podcasts play a crucial role in educating the public about Sasquatch research, dispelling myths, and presenting evidence-based discussions. By providing accurate information and engaging storytelling, podcasts contribute to a more informed and open-minded public perception of Sasquatch, challenging preconceived notions and encouraging critical thinking. Through personal stories, interviews, and expert discussions, podcasts help break down the stigma associated with Sasquatch research and eyewitness accounts. By presenting credible and compelling narratives, podcasts contribute to the normalization of Sasquatch encounters, encouraging individuals to approach the subject with curiosity and respect.

In some ways, podcasts have revolutionized the way Sasquatch research is conducted, shared, and perceived. Through their accessibility, community-building capabilities, and ability to provide validation and support, podcasts have empowered witnesses to come forward and share their encounters, while also fostering collaboration among researchers. By disseminating research, challenging stigmas, and educating the public, podcasts have played a vital role in advancing our understanding of Sasquatch and shaping a more inclusive and informed discourse surrounding this enigmatic creature. As the podcasting medium continues to evolve, it holds immense potential for furthering Sasquatch research and inspiring new generations of researchers and witnesses to explore this field.

Storytelling and Validation

Sasquatch encounter podcasts provide a platform for individuals to share their own experiences and encounters. By sharing these stories, podcast hosts and guests create a sense of validation for listeners who have had similar experiences. This storytelling aspect can encourage individuals to come forward and report their own encounters, knowing that they will be heard and understood by a community of like-minded individuals. Storytelling has been an integral part of human culture since time immemorial.

In the realm of Sasquatch research, storytelling plays a crucial role in shaping the community, validating witnesses' experiences, and preserving the rich history of encounters. Native American and First Nations cultures have a long-standing tradition of passing down stories and legends about Sasquatch through oral traditions. These stories serve as a valuable source of knowledge, providing insights into Sasquatch behavior, habitat, and interactions with humans, which can inform contemporary research efforts.

Storytelling fosters a sense of community among Sasquatch researchers, enthusiasts, and witnesses by creating a shared narrative and a space for individuals to connect and relate to one another. By sharing their encounters and experiences, individuals find validation, support, and a sense of belonging within the Bigfoot research community. Witnesses of Sasquatch encounters often face skepticism and ridicule from mainstream society. Through storytelling, witnesses find validation and support from others who have had similar experiences, helping them overcome the stigma associated with their encounters.

Sharing their stories allows witnesses to process their encounters, find closure, and heal from any emotional distress caused by their experiences. Validation from the research community empowers witnesses, giving them the confidence to come forward and contribute to the collective knowledge of Sasquatch.

Native American and First Nations stories about Sasquatch hold immense cultural significance, often portraying these creatures as spiritual beings or guardians of the natural world. These stories reflect a deep connection between indigenous communities and the land, emphasizing the importance of respecting and coexisting with Sasquatch.

These stories provide valuable historical knowledge about Sasquatch encounters, dating back centuries or even millennia. By incorporating this historical knowledge into contemporary research, we can gain a broader understanding of Sasquatch behavior and its significance within indigenous cultures.

The storytelling traditions of Native American and First Nations people offer a unique perspective that can complement scientific research. By bridging traditional knowledge with scientific methodologies, researchers can gain a more holistic understanding of Sasquatch, incorporating both empirical evidence and indigenous wisdom.

In addition to oral traditions, storytelling has found new platforms in the digital age, such as podcasts, blogs, and social media. These platforms provide a wider reach, allowing witnesses and researchers to share their stories with a global audience, fostering greater awareness and understanding of Sasquatch encounters.

The continuation of storytelling ensures the preservation of indigenous cultures and their unique perspectives on Sasquatch. By honoring and respecting these stories, we can preserve the cultural heritage of Native American and First Nations people while advancing our knowledge of Sasquatch.

Storytelling and validation play a vital role in shaping the Bigfoot research community. By sharing their encounters and experiences, witnesses find validation, support, and healing, overcoming skepticism and stigma. The parallels between Native American and First Nations stories and contemporary Sasquatch research highlight the importance of incorporating traditional knowledge into scientific investigations. As storytelling continues to evolve through modern platforms, it ensures the preservation of cultural heritage and contributes to a more comprehensive understanding of Sasquatch. By embracing the power of storytelling and validation, we can foster a stronger sense of community, encourage witnesses to come forward and advance our knowledge of this elusive creature.

Community Engagement and Support

Sasquatch encounter podcasts foster a sense of community among listeners who share an interest in the subject. Listeners can engage with hosts, guests, and fellow enthusiasts through social media platforms, forums, and live events. This sense of community provides a supportive environment for individuals to share their encounters, seek advice, and find validation. The encouragement and support from this community may embolden individuals to report their own sightings, contributing to the increase in reported encounters.

The popularity of Sasquatch encounter podcasts can also influence psychological factors that contribute to an increase in reported sightings. As we have already discussed, the power of suggestion, availability heuristic, and social contagion can all come into play. Listeners who are exposed to numerous accounts of Sasquatch encounters may be more likely to interpret their own experiences as evidence of Sasquatch's existence, influenced by the stories they have heard.

While it is challenging to establish a direct causal relationship between Sasquatch encounter podcasts and Sasquatch's popularity in pop culture with the increase in reported sightings, there are compelling arguments to suggest their influence. The power of suggestion, the availability heuristic, social contagion, and increased awareness and reporting channels all contribute to the complex dynamics surrounding Sasquatch sightings. The media exposure and awareness generated by podcasts, along with the storytelling and validation they provide, contribute to a sense of community engagement and support. These factors, combined with psychological influences, can fuel the fire of reported Sasquatch encounters.

As the popularity of Sasquatch encounter podcasts continues to grow and Sasquatch continues to capture the public's imagination through books, movies, and television shows, it is essential to approach reported sightings with critical thinking and skepticism. While some sightings may indeed be genuine, others may be influenced by cultural factors and psychological biases. By maintaining a balanced perspective and applying rigorous investigation, researchers can navigate the intricate relationship between Sasquatch's popularity in pop culture and the frequency of reported sightings, ultimately striving towards a deeper understanding of this enduring mysterious phenomenon.

5

UNVEILING THE HOAXES:
INFAMOUS SASQUATCH DECEPTIONS

While the legend of Sasquatch has captivated the imaginations of many, it has also been plagued by numerous hoaxes throughout the years. In this chapter, we will delve into some of the most well-known and proven Sasquatch hoaxes of the last several decades. By examining the facts and details of each incident, we can shed light on the deceptive practices that have clouded the search for the truth behind these elusive creatures.

One of the earliest and most infamous Sasquatch hoaxes involved the alleged footprints discovered by a worker employed by Ray Wallace in 1958. Ray Wallace, a construction worker from Washington State, was a notorious prankster who, upon his death in 2002, was posthumously credited by his family with creating the Sasquatch phenomenon. According to his family, Wallace used wooden stompers to create the infamous Sasquatch tracks that have captivated the public's imagination for decades. However, the claim that Wallace was responsible for all the alleged Sasquatch tracks has been met with skepticism and controversy within the research community.

The argument against Wallace being responsible for all the tracks primarily revolves around the sheer number and geographical spread of Sasquatch sightings and track discoveries. Sasquatch sightings and track findings have been reported across North America, from Florida to California, and from British Columbia to New York. It would have been logistically impossible for Wallace to have traveled to all these locations and created all the tracks himself.

Many of the tracks attributed to Sasquatch do not match the wooden stompers produced by Wallace's family. The wooden stompers are flat, lacking the depth and contour of a real foot. In contrast, many of the tracks show signs of flexibility and movement, such as toe splaying, mid-tarsal break, and dermal ridges, which could not have been produced by a rigid wooden stomper.

The size and shape of the tracks also vary significantly. While Wallace's stompers measure 16 inches in length, some tracks have been found that range from 12 to 24 inches in length. The tracks also differ in width, toe number, and toe arrangement, suggesting that they were made by different individuals or species.

The foot casts themselves provide compelling evidence against Wallace's claim. Many of the casts show anatomical features that are consistent with a living, bipedal primate, not a wooden stomper. These features include a flexible foot structure, a non-human toe arrangement, and dermal ridges that match the friction ridges found on primate feet.

While Ray Wallace may have contributed to the Sasquatch phenomenon with his wooden stompers, the evidence suggests that he was not responsible for all the tracks attributed to Bigfoot. The diversity and complexity of the tracks, the geographical spread of the sightings, and the anatomical details of the foot casts all point to the existence of an unknown, bipedal primate in North America.

The Rick Dyer Georgia Sasquatch hoax is one of the most infamous hoaxes in the history of Bigfoot sightings. It took place in 2008 and involved two men, Rick Dyer and Matthew Whitton, who claimed to have discovered the body of a Sasquatch in the woods of Georgia.

Rick Dyer, a former corrections officer, and Matthew Whitton, a former police officer, announced in July 2008 that they had found the body in the northern mountains of Georgia. They claimed to have stumbled upon the creature while hiking and decided to bring it back to civilization. They released photos of the alleged creature, which they claimed was over 7 feet tall and weighed over 500 pounds.

The two men held a press conference in Palo Alto, California, where they presented their evidence to the world. They showed a freezer containing what appeared to be a large, hairy creature. They also presented a video of their discovery, which they claimed showed the creature moving.

The story quickly gained international attention, with media outlets around the world reporting on the alleged discovery. However, skeptics immediately questioned the authenticity of the evidence. Many pointed out that the creature in the freezer looked suspiciously like a costume, and the video was criticized for its poor quality and lack of clear footage of the creature.

Despite the skepticism, Dyer and Whitton stood by their claims. They even sold the alleged Bigfoot body to Tom Biscardi, a well-known Bigfoot enthusiast and promoter, for an undisclosed amount. Biscardi announced plans to conduct scientific tests on the body to prove its authenticity.

But the hoax began to unravel when the body was thawed for examination. The creature was revealed to be a rubber suit filled with animal parts and other materials. The revelation led to widespread ridicule and condemnation of Dyer, Whitton, and Biscardi.

Whitton was subsequently fired from his job as a police officer, and Dyer faced significant backlash from the public. Biscardi claimed that he had been deceived by Dyer and Whitton and sued them for fraud. However, the lawsuit was later dropped.

Despite the fallout from the hoax, Dyer continued to claim that he had encountered Sasquatch. In 2012, he announced that he had killed a Sasquatch in Texas, but this claim was also widely dismissed as a hoax.

The Rick Dyer Georgia Sasquatch hoax serves as a cautionary tale about the dangers of deception and the importance of skepticism. Despite the initial excitement and media attention, the hoax ultimately led to significant consequences for those involved and did nothing to further the search for Sasquatch.

Psychological Characteristics Behind Sasquatch Deception

These hoaxes leave us, the enthusiasts and researchers, questioning the motivations behind these deceptive acts. Human beings are innately curious creatures. From the moment we develop cognitive abilities, we start to question the world around us. One of the most profound aspects of this curiosity is our desire to understand why people do what they do.

The desire to understand motivations is rooted in our evolutionary history. As social animals, early humans needed to predict and understand the behavior of others in their group to survive and thrive. Understanding motivations allowed them to anticipate actions, avoid conflicts, and foster cooperation. This evolutionary perspective is supported by numerous studies in anthropology and psychology, suggesting that our brains are wired to seek out and understand the motivations of others.

This quest for understanding motivations is not just about survival. It's also about creating meaningful connections and building empathy. When we understand why someone acts in a certain way, we can empathize with their situation, feelings, and perspectives. This empathy strengthens our social bonds and fosters a sense of community and belonging.

Our desire to understand motivations also extends to our self-awareness. By understanding our motivations, we gain insight into our behaviors, emotions, and thoughts. This self-understanding is crucial for personal growth and self-improvement. It allows us to make conscious decisions, regulate our emotions, and strive towards our goals.

The drive for understanding motivations is also a cornerstone of many disciplines, from psychology and sociology to literature and philosophy. In psychology, for instance, understanding motivations is key to diagnosing and treating mental health disorders. In sociology, it helps explain social phenomena and guide policymaking. In literature and philosophy, it provides a deeper understanding of human nature and the human condition.

But the fact is, understanding motivations is not always straightforward. People's motivations can be complex, multifaceted, and sometimes hidden even from themselves. They can be influenced by a myriad of factors, from biological needs and psychological drives to social pressures and cultural norms. Above all, motivations can change over time and in different contexts.

Despite these challenges, our quest for understanding motivations is relentless. We continue to develop theories, conduct research, and create tools to better understand why people do what they do. This reflects our deep-seated desire to make sense of our world, connect with others, and understand ourselves.

Therefore, I would like to examine some of the psychological characteristics and personality traits that may contribute to people hoaxing Sasquatch encounters and evidence. By looking at the underlying motivations and psychological factors, we may gain insights into the complex mindset of those who perpetrate these hoaxes.

Attention-Seeking

One prominent psychological characteristic that may drive individuals to hoax Sasquatch encounters is a desire for attention. Some individuals crave recognition and validation, and by fabricating Sasquatch sightings or evidence, they can achieve a temporary sense of notoriety. The attention garnered from media, social media, and the Bigfoot community can be a powerful motivator for those seeking recognition and validation. The attention-seeking psychological characteristic refers to a pattern of behavior in individuals who actively seek attention, validation, and recognition from others. These individuals often engage in various actions or behaviors to draw attention to themselves, often at the expense of truth or authenticity. When it comes to faking Sasquatch evidence or encounters, this attention-seeking characteristic can play a key role in motivating individuals to fabricate or exaggerate their claims.

Attention-seeking individuals have an intense desire to be noticed, acknowledged, and admired by others. They often feel a sense of emptiness or inadequacy and believe that gaining attention will fill this void. Faking Sasquatch evidence or encounters provides a unique opportunity for attention-seekers, as the subject of Sasquatch has captivated public interest for decades. By fabricating evidence or encounters, they can attract media attention, gain followers, or become the center of public fascination.

Attention-seekers often crave validation and recognition from others. They may feel a lack of self-worth or struggle with low self-esteem, leading them to seek external validation as a means of boosting their self-image. Faking Sasquatch evidence or encounters allows them to present themselves as knowledgeable or special, as they claim to have encountered or discovered something extraordinary. The validation they receive from others reinforces their sense of self-worth and feeds their attention-seeking behavior.

Attention-seekers often strive for social status and recognition within their communities or social circles. By faking Sasquatch evidence or encounters, they position themselves as experts or authorities in the field, gaining respect and admiration from others who are interested in the subject. This elevated social status fulfills their need for recognition and reinforces their attention-seeking behavior.

Some attention-seekers derive pleasure or excitement from deceiving others. The act of fabricating evidence or encounters can provide a sense of power, control, or superiority over those who believe their claims. This thrill of deception can be a motivating factor for individuals who fake Sasquatch evidence, as they enjoy the attention and reactions they receive from others when their fabricated stories are believed.

Attention-seeking behavior can also serve as a means of escaping from personal problems or difficulties. By immersing themselves in the world of Sasquatch, attention-seekers can temporarily divert attention from their own challenges and focus on the attention and validation they receive from others. Faking evidence or encounters allows them to create a fantasy world where they are the center of attention, providing a temporary escape from their own reality.

It is important to note that not all individuals who present Sasquatch evidence or encounters are attention-seekers or intentionally deceptive. Some may genuinely believe in their experiences, while others may be influenced by misperceptions, hoaxes, or psychological factors unrelated to attention-seeking behavior. However, for those who do exhibit attention-seeking characteristics, the desire for attention, validation, social status, the thrill of deception, and escapism can all contribute to their motivation to fake Sasquatch evidence or encounters.

Prankster Mentality

For some individuals, the act of hoaxing Sasquatch encounters may stem from a mischievous or prankster mentality. These individuals may find enjoyment in deceiving others, creating elaborate hoaxes to elicit reactions and amusement. The thrill of fooling others and the sense of control over the narrative can be enticing for those with a prankster mindset. The prankster mentality psychological characteristic refers to a specific mindset or personality trait that drives individuals to engage in pranks, hoaxes, or practical jokes. It involves a strong inclination towards creating and perpetuating deceptive or misleading situations for the purpose of amusement, entertainment, or personal satisfaction. This characteristic can manifest in various ways, including the creation of fake evidence or encounters related to mythical creatures like Sasquatch.

Individuals with a prankster mentality often possess a mischievous nature and derive pleasure from fooling others. They may have a strong desire to elicit reactions, create confusion, or simply enjoy the thrill of deceiving others. This psychological characteristic can be seen as an expression of creativity, as pranksters often invest time and effort into crafting elaborate hoaxes or fabricating evidence that appears convincing.

When it comes to faking Sasquatch evidence or encounters, the prankster mentality plays a key role in several aspects. Firstly, individuals with this characteristic may be motivated by the desire to generate attention or notoriety. By creating fake evidence or encounters, they can attract media attention, gain followers or fans, or simply enjoy the sense of accomplishment that comes from successfully fooling others.

Secondly, the prankster mentality allows individuals to tap into the fascination and intrigue surrounding mythical creatures like Sasquatch. By fabricating evidence or encounters, they can contribute to the ongoing debate and speculation about the existence of such creatures. This can be particularly appealing to those who enjoy stirring up controversy or challenging established beliefs.

Finally, the prankster mentality often thrives on the reactions and responses of others. When individuals fake Sasquatch evidence or encounters, they anticipate the excitement, skepticism, or even fear that their actions may elicit. The ability to provoke strong emotional responses in others can be highly rewarding for pranksters, as it reinforces their sense of accomplishment and feeds their desire for amusement.

It is important to note that while the prankster mentality may explain the motivations behind faking Sasquatch evidence or encounters, it does not justify or excuse such behavior. Fabricating evidence or perpetuating hoaxes can have negative consequences, including misleading the public, wasting resources, and undermining genuine scientific research. Additionally, it can erode trust and credibility within the field of cryptozoology, making it more challenging for legitimate researchers to be taken seriously.

While this may explain the motivations behind such actions, it is important to recognize the potential negative consequences and ethical implications associated with fabricating evidence or perpetuating hoaxes.

Financial Gain

In certain cases, financial gain serves as a significant motivator for individuals to hoax Sasquatch encounters and evidence. Hoaxers may see an opportunity to profit from their deception, whether through selling books, or merchandise, or charging fees for viewing alleged evidence. The allure of financial gain can be a powerful driving force for those who prioritize personal gain over the pursuit of truth. The financial gain associated with fabricating Sasquatch evidence or making up encounters can be a significant motivator for some individuals. This motivation can be broken down into several key areas: media attention, merchandise sales, tourism, and research funding.

Stories about Sasquatch sightings or evidence can attract significant media attention, which can lead to financial gain. This can come in the form of paid interviews, book deals, or even movie rights. For example, the Patterson-Gimlin film has reportedly earned its creators significant income through licensing and other related ventures.

Fabricated evidence or encounters can also lead to opportunities for merchandise sales. This can include everything from t-shirts and mugs to books and DVDs. Some individuals have even created entire brands around their alleged encounters or evidence.

In areas where Sasquatch sightings are common, fabricated evidence or encounters can boost local tourism. This can lead to increased income for local businesses, and some individuals may even be able to charge for tours or other Sasquatch-related experiences.

Some individuals may fabricate evidence or encounters in order to secure funding for further research. This can come from private donors, crowdfunding campaigns, or even grants in some cases.

In the digital age, the line between reality and fiction often blurs, especially on social media platforms like YouTube, Instagram, and Facebook. One such example is the phenomenon of hoaxing Sasquatch evidence, a practice that has not only gained significant attention but also translated into real money for the hoaxers. The intricate process of creating and promoting hoaxed Sasquatch evidence, creating clickbait headlines attracting viewers, and the monetization strategies that turn these hoaxes into profitable ventures often drive hoaxers to do what they do.

The first step in the process is the creation of the hoax itself. This typically involves producing a video or a series of photographs that purportedly show evidence of Sasquatch. The hoaxer might use costumes, props, or digital editing techniques to create a convincing illusion. The goal is to create content that is just believable enough to pique the curiosity of viewers, but not so obviously fake that it is immediately dismissed.

Once the hoax is created, the next step is to promote it on social media platforms. This is where the concept of clickbait comes into play. Clickbait refers to sensational or misleading headlines designed to attract clicks and drive traffic to a particular webpage or video. In the case of Sasquatch hoaxes, these headlines might include phrases like "Shocking Bigfoot Sighting Caught on Tape!" or "Real Sasquatch Evidence Uncovered!" The more sensational and intriguing the headline, the more likely it is to attract viewers.

The role of social media algorithms cannot be understated in this process. Platforms like YouTube and Instagram use complex algorithms to determine what content to show to users. These algorithms often prioritize content that generates high engagement, including likes, shares, and comments. Therefore, a hoax video with a clickbait headline that attracts a lot of views and engagement is likely to be promoted by the platform's algorithm, leading to even more views.

The final piece of the puzzle is monetization. On platforms like YouTube, creators can earn money through ad revenue. The more views a video gets, the more ads can be shown, and the more money the creator can potentially earn. Some creators also use Patreon or other crowdfunding platforms to earn money directly from their viewers. In addition, hoaxers might sell merchandise related to their hoax, such as t-shirts or mugs featuring images of the supposed Sasquatch.

However, it's important to note that while this process can be profitable, it's also ethically dubious. Hoaxing Sasquatch evidence and using clickbait headlines to attract viewers is a form of deception. It exploits people's curiosity and desire for the extraordinary, and it can contribute to the spread of misinformation online. Ultimately it can and often does undermine the credibility of genuine researchers and enthusiasts in the field of cryptozoology.

The phenomenon of hoaxing Sasquatch evidence for clickbait and revenue is a complex process that involves the creation of convincing hoaxes, the use of sensational headlines to attract viewers and various monetization strategies. While it can be profitable, it's also a practice that raises significant ethical concerns.

It's also important to note that while these financial incentives can motivate some individuals to fabricate evidence or encounters, not all Sasquatch sightings or evidence are hoaxes. Many people who report sightings or find evidence genuinely believe in what they've seen or found. Additionally, fabricating evidence or encounters can have serious consequences, including damage to one's reputation and potential legal repercussions.

Psychological Need for Belonging

Some individuals may hoax Sasquatch encounters as a means to fulfill a psychological need for belonging. By fabricating sightings or evidence, they can gain acceptance and validation within the Bigfoot community or among like-minded individuals. The desire to be part of a group and to feel a sense of belonging can be a compelling motivator for those who feel disconnected or seek social validation. The psychological need for belonging is a fundamental human motivation, deeply rooted in our evolutionary history. This need is so powerful that it can drive individuals to engage in a variety of behaviors, including the creation of hoaxes or false claims about Sasquatch sightings.

This analysis will delve into the intricate relationship between the need for belonging and the phenomenon of Sasquatch hoaxes. The need for belonging, as defined by psychologists, is the inherent desire to form and maintain strong, stable interpersonal relationships. It is a universal human experience, and when this need is not met, it can lead to feelings of loneliness, depression, and anxiety. In the context of Sasquatch hoaxes, this need for belonging can manifest in several ways.

Firstly, the creation of a Sasquatch hoax or false claim can provide an individual with a sense of belonging to a specific community, in this case, the community of Sasquatch believers. This community is characterized by shared beliefs, common interests, and mutual support, all of which can fulfill an individual's need for belonging. By creating a hoax or false claim, an individual can gain acceptance, recognition, and a sense of belonging within this community.

Secondly, the act of creating a Sasquatch hoax or false claim can also serve as a form of social bonding. The planning, execution, and subsequent sharing of the hoax or false claim can involve collaboration with others, which can foster a sense of camaraderie and shared purpose. This can further satisfy an individual's need for belonging.

Thirdly, the creation of a Sasquatch hoax or false claim can provide an individual with a sense of identity. By aligning themselves with the Sasquatch believer community, individuals can construct a unique identity that sets them apart from the mainstream. This identity can provide a sense of belonging, as it connects them with a group of like-minded individuals.

However, it's important to note that while the need for belonging can drive individuals to create Sasquatch hoaxes or false claims, it does not justify these actions. Hoaxes and false claims can cause harm, spread misinformation, and undermine the credibility of legitimate research. Therefore, while understanding the psychological motivations behind these behaviors is important, it is equally important to promote critical thinking, skepticism, and scientific literacy to prevent the spread of hoaxes and false claims.

The psychological need for belonging plays a significant role in the phenomenon of Sasquatch hoaxes and false claims. By providing a sense of community, social bonding, and identity, these behaviors can fulfill an individual's need for belonging. However, the potential harm caused by these behaviors underscores the importance of promoting critical thinking and scientific literacy.

Psychological Thrill

For a subset of individuals, the act of hoaxing Sasquatch encounters may provide a psychological thrill. The planning, execution, and subsequent reactions to their deception can create a sense of excitement and adrenaline. The psychological thrill derived from deceiving others and manipulating their beliefs can be a driving force for those who enjoy the challenge and excitement of engaging in elaborate hoaxes.

The psychological thrill personality trait refers to an individual's tendency to seek out, engage in, and enjoy activities that are exciting, adventurous, and potentially risky. This trait is often associated with sensation-seeking behavior, which is characterized by the pursuit of novel and intense experiences without regard for physical, social, legal, or financial risk. Individuals with this trait may be drawn to the excitement and risk associated with creating a hoax or telling a false story. They may enjoy the challenge of creating convincing evidence or a believable narrative, as well as the thrill of potentially fooling others.

These individuals may also be motivated by the potential attention and recognition they could receive if their hoax or story is believed. The prospect of becoming the center of attention, even temporarily, can be very appealing to those with a psychological thrill personality trait. They may also derive satisfaction from the sense of power and control they feel when they manipulate others' beliefs and perceptions.

The psychological thrill personality trait can influence the way these individuals perceive and respond to potential consequences. They may downplay or disregard the risks associated with their actions, focusing instead on the potential rewards. This can lead them to take actions that others might consider reckless or irresponsible.

It is important to remember again, that not everyone who hoaxes Sasquatch evidence or fabricates encounter stories necessarily has a psychological thrill personality trait. Other factors, such as a desire for financial gain, a need for validation, or a belief in the existence of Sasquatch, can also motivate these behaviors.

While the psychological thrill personality trait can contribute to these behaviors, it doesn't necessarily lead to them. Many people with this trait engage in thrill-seeking behaviors that are legal, socially acceptable, and not harmful to others.

The psychological thrill personality trait can certainly play a significant role in individuals' decisions to hoax Sasquatch evidence or make up encounter stories. However, it's just one of many factors that can influence these behaviors, and its presence doesn't guarantee that an individual will engage in such actions.

The Narcissistic Influence on Sasquatch Hoaxes

Narcissistic Personality Disorder (NPD) is a mental condition characterized by an inflated sense of self-importance, a deep need for excessive attention and admiration, troubled relationships, and a lack of empathy for others. I think we should take a look at the intriguing intersection of NPD and the phenomenon of faking Sasquatch experiences or hoaxing Sasquatch evidence such as photos and videos.

The connection between NPD and Sasquatch hoaxes may not be immediately apparent, but a closer examination reveals a fascinating interplay. Individuals with NPD often seek to be the center of attention and may resort to extreme measures to achieve this. Faking a Sasquatch sighting or creating false evidence can provide a platform for such individuals to gain the attention and admiration they crave.

The Narcissistic Need for Attention and Admiration

Narcissistic individuals have an insatiable need for attention and admiration. They often feel superior to others and believe they are unique and special. This can lead them to seek out extraordinary experiences or claim unique knowledge that sets them apart from the crowd. In the context of Sasquatch sightings, a narcissistic individual may fabricate an encounter or evidence to position themselves as a special figure in the Bigfoot community. They may relish the attention and admiration that comes with being a "witness" or "discoverer" of such a rare and elusive creature.

Manipulation and Deception

Narcissists are often skilled manipulators and can be deceitful to maintain their self-image or to gain attention. They may create elaborate stories or hoaxes, such as faking Sasquatch sightings or evidence, to manipulate others into giving them the attention they crave. The more elaborate the hoax, the more attention it is likely to garner, feeding the narcissist's need for admiration.

Narcissists are often adept at manipulation and deception, skills they use to maintain their inflated self-image and to gain the attention and admiration they crave. When it comes to hoaxing Sasquatch evidence or faking videos or photographs, they may employ a variety of tactics.

Narcissists may weave intricate narratives around their fake evidence. They might describe in great detail their encounter with Sasquatch, using vivid and compelling language to make their story more believable. They may also incorporate elements that make them appear brave, knowledgeable, or special in some way, further feeding their need for admiration.

Narcissists may go to great lengths to create convincing fake evidence. This could involve using props, costumes, or special effects to create a realistic-looking Sasquatch in photos or videos. They might also manipulate images or footage using digital tools to make their hoax more convincing.

Narcissists can be skilled at playing on people's emotions to manipulate them. They might use fear, excitement, or curiosity to draw people in and make them more likely to believe their hoax. For example, they might describe their fake Sasquatch encounter as a terrifying or awe-inspiring experience, playing on people's fear of the unknown or their fascination with the mysterious.

Once they've launched their hoax, narcissists will often work hard to maintain the deception. They might vehemently defend their evidence against skeptics, using persuasive arguments or even attacking the credibility of those who question them. They may also seek out supportive individuals or communities who are more likely to believe their stories, further reinforcing their deception.

In all these ways, narcissists use manipulation and deception to create and maintain their Sasquatch hoaxes. Their ultimate goal is to gain the attention and admiration they crave, and they are often willing to go to great lengths to achieve this.

Lack of Empathy

A key characteristic of NPD is a lack of empathy for others. This can manifest in a disregard for the feelings or interests of others. In the context of Sasquatch hoaxes, narcissistic individuals may not consider or care about the impact of their actions on the Bigfoot research community or the public at large. They may not empathize with the disappointment or disillusionment that can result when a hoax is revealed.

When a narcissistic individual decides to fake Sasquatch evidence or create a hoax, they are primarily focused on their own needs - the need for attention, admiration, and validation. They are not considering the impact of their actions on others. By creating fake evidence or hoaxes, narcissists can mislead the public and create false beliefs or fears. They may not consider or care about the confusion, disappointment, or even fear that their actions might cause.

Sasquatch hoaxes can undermine genuine research efforts. They can create skepticism and cynicism, making it harder for legitimate researchers to gain support or credibility. Narcissists may not empathize with the frustration and challenges this can cause for these researchers.

The Bigfoot community is often a target of ridicule and skepticism. Hoaxes can further damage the community's credibility and make it harder for those who are genuinely interested in the existence of Sasquatch to be taken seriously. Narcissists may not consider or care about this impact.

For those who are genuinely interested in the existence of Sasquatch, being misled by a hoax can cause emotional distress. They may feel disappointed, betrayed, or even foolish for believing in the hoax. A narcissist may not empathize with these feelings. This disregard for others is a key factor in their willingness and ability to create and maintain these hoaxes.

The Role of Social Media

In today's digital age, social media provides a perfect platform for narcissistic individuals to gain the attention they crave. By posting fake Sasquatch photos or videos, they can quickly attract a large audience and receive instant feedback in the form of likes, shares, and comments. This immediate gratification can further fuel their narcissistic tendencies and encourage more elaborate hoaxes.

Social media platforms like Facebook, Instagram, Twitter, and YouTube offer a global stage for individuals to share their experiences and perspectives. For narcissists, these platforms provide an opportunity to gain the attention and admiration they crave. They can create a carefully curated persona that highlights their perceived uniqueness and superiority. In the context of Sasquatch hoaxes, social media allows narcissists to share their fabricated encounters or fake evidence with a wide audience, garnering likes, shares, and comments that feed their need for validation.

Narcissists may use various tools and techniques to create convincing fake Sasquatch evidence. This could involve using props, costumes, or special effects to create a realistic-looking Sasquatch in photos or videos. They might also manipulate images or footage using digital tools to make their hoax more convincing. Once the evidence is created, they can easily share it on social media platforms, where it can quickly gain traction and spread.

In addition to creating fake evidence, narcissists may also craft elaborate Sasquatch encounter stories. They might weave intricate narratives that position them as brave, knowledgeable, or special. These stories can be shared in written form on platforms like Facebook or Twitter or narrated in videos on YouTube. The interactive nature of social media allows narcissists to engage with their audience, respond to comments, and further embellish their stories.

Narcissists often use persuasive language, emotional appeals, and strategic timing to make their hoaxes more believable. They may also create fake accounts to support their claims, and the anonymity and distance provided by social media can make it easier for narcissists to deceive others and maintain their hoaxes.

While social media can enable narcissistic Sasquatch hoaxes, it can also amplify their impact. Fake evidence and false stories can spread quickly and widely, reaching a global audience. This can create confusion and spread misinformation.

It certainly underscores the importance of critical thinking and skepticism in evaluating Sasquatch sightings and evidence while also highlighting the need for empathy and understanding in dealing with individuals who may be struggling with mental health issues.

As we have discovered, the motivations behind hoaxing Sasquatch encounters and evidence are complex and varied, influenced by a range of psychological characteristics and personality traits. Attention-seeking, a prankster mentality, financial gain, the psychological need for belonging, and the psychological thrill of deception all contribute to the mindset of those who perpetrate these hoaxes.

Understanding the underlying motivations can help researchers and enthusiasts approach Sasquatch evidence with critical thinking and skepticism. By recognizing the potential psychological factors at play, we, the Bigfoot community, can better navigate the landscape of hoaxes and focus on genuine evidence and credible research. Ultimately, by shedding light on the psychological characteristics behind Sasquatch deception, we can strive towards a more authentic and rigorous investigation of the elusive creature.

As the search for Sasquatch continues, it is crucial to approach evidence with a critical eye, separating fact from fiction. By learning from the mistakes of the past and maintaining a commitment to scientific rigor, researchers can strive towards uncovering the truth behind the legend of Sasquatch, free from the shadow of hoaxes and deception.

6

FIELD RESEARCH:
MY JOURNEY TO RADIUM

Todd Standing, a Sasquatch investigator hailing from Calgary, Alberta, is renowned for his high-resolution, close-range footage, captured in the full light of day, of what he claims to be Sasquatches. In 2017, Standing showcased his videos in his documentary, *Discovering Bigfoot*.

The following is a comprehensive description of the film, sourced from the *Discovering Bigfoot* IMDB page.

"*Discovering Bigfoot* is the first feature film documentary with real live interaction between a Bigfoot creature, wilderness experts, PhDs, and other world-renowned experts and researchers of the Bigfoot enigma. Journey into the heart of Sasquatch Country with Todd Standing who appeared with *Survivorman*'s Les Stroud in *Survivorman: Bigfoot*. Experience three incredible days in the field with Bigfoot researchers, Todd Standing and renowned expert Professor Dr. Jeff Meldrum as they encounter a real live Sasquatch. What we think we know of human origins and evolution is about to change forever as we discover the truth about a species that has remained elusive by outwitting and evading modern man for decades despite his best efforts. New evidence is revealed through scientific, systematic, and logical processes proving the existence of the Sasquatch species, a modern-day descendant of *Gigantopithicus*, a.k.a. Bigfoot. This unprecedented feature film includes - Never before seen, extraordinary Sasquatch footage that will shock the world. A terrifying altercation between Todd Standing and 3 Sasquatch creatures in the wild. Five never-before-seen video encounters with the Sasquatch species and an overview of the life and death struggle that was necessary to acquire them. YOU WILL FEEL THE FEAR."

Standing, made headlines in 2017 when he filed a lawsuit against the governments of British Columbia and Alberta in Canada. Standing sought to have the Sasquatch, officially recognized as a species by the Canadian government.

In his lawsuit, Standing claimed that the governments of British Columbia and Alberta were "in dereliction of their duty" for not recognizing the existence of the Sasquatch, despite what he claimed was overwhelming evidence. He argued that the government's refusal to acknowledge the Sasquatch was causing harm to the public and to the Sasquatch species itself. He also claimed that the government was infringing on his rights and freedoms by not recognizing the Sasquatch.

Standing's lawsuit was based on his own experiences and research, which he claimed provided irrefutable evidence of the Sasquatch's existence. He cited his own sightings and encounters with the creature, as well as physical evidence such as footprints, videos, and hair samples. He also pointed to eyewitness accounts and historical reports as further proof of the Sasquatch's existence.

The lawsuit was met with skepticism by many, including the legal community and the mainstream media. Critics pointed out that Standing's evidence was largely anecdotal and lacked scientific rigor. They also questioned his motives, suggesting that the lawsuit was a publicity stunt to promote his documentary, "Discovering Bigfoot."

The courts ultimately dismissed Standing's lawsuit. In his ruling, Justice Kenneth Ball of the Supreme Court of British Columbia stated that the case was not a matter for the courts to decide, but rather a scientific issue that should be addressed by the scientific community.

The reaction within the Sasquatch research community was mixed. Some supported Standing's efforts to bring attention to the Sasquatch phenomenon and applauded his boldness in taking legal action. Others, however, criticized his approach, arguing that it lacked scientific rigor and undermined the credibility of Sasquatch research.

Despite the dismissal of his lawsuit, Standing remains committed to his cause. He continues to advocate for the recognition of the Sasquatch as a species and to conduct research in hopes of providing definitive proof of its existence.

I first watched Todd's documentary towards the end of 2019. My initial reaction to his videos was that they seemed to be authentic. I was astounded and puzzled as to why the Bigfoot community wasn't buzzing about this incredible footage. As I looked deeper into it, I discovered that many people were indeed discussing it.

There were two main perspectives on Todd Standing and his videos. Some firmly believed that the videos were entirely genuine, asserting that Todd had successfully captured multiple Sasquatches in broad daylight, on multiple occasions, in different locations, and all in high definition. Yet there were others who were convinced that the videos were merely sophisticated fakes and that Standing was a hoaxer.

Unsure of what to believe, I rewatched the documentary and the individual videos. I scrutinized them repeatedly, focusing on the minute details of the videos and Standing himself. The more I examined the videos and the figures in them, the more skeptical I became. Todd himself seemed rather self-absorbed, and he made numerous unverified claims about his background in his documentary.

During his on-screen interactions with Dr. Jeff Meldrum and the late Dr. John Bindernagel, it seemed as though Standing was guiding them toward his desired conclusions. Both appeared to have had experiences while in the wilderness with Todd, but neither could definitively link those experiences to Sasquatch. Gradually, my views on Standing and his videos shifted, and I became convinced that his videos were likely sophisticated hoaxes rather than genuine Sasquatch footage.

In addition to Meldrum and Bindernagel, Todd also spent time with Les Stroud, a Canadian survival expert, filmmaker, and accomplished musician, best known as the creator and star of the hit TV series *Survivorman*. In 2013 and 2014, Stroud and Standing filmed episodes of Stroud's YouTube series *Survivorman Bigfoot*. During the filming, Stroud had several experiences that couldn't be easily dismissed as hoaxes.

I am a big fan of *Survivorman* and have a great deal of respect for Les Stroud, both for his survival skills and his immersive filmmaking. After spending time with Todd, Stroud seemed to have developed a mutual respect for him. This bothered me a bit. If Todd was indeed a hoaxer, how could he deceive not one, but two PhD professors and a straight-talking guy like Les Stroud? Was I overlooking something?

Determined to uncover the truth, I invited Dr. Jeff Meldrum and Les Stroud onto my *Sasquatch Odyssey* podcast. Dr. Meldrum did appear on the show, but we ran out of time before we could discuss his time with Todd Standing. However, I recently had the opportunity to ask him about it over dinner at an event in Idaho.

He said he liked Todd and couldn't explain his experiences during the filming of the *Discovering Bigfoot* documentary. Although he couldn't definitively label any of his experiences as hoaxes, he couldn't say that he had interacted with nor witnessed a Sasquatch.

It took quite a bit longer to get Les Stroud on the show, but in October of 2021, we sat down for an in-depth interview. After around thirty minutes, I asked Les about his time with Todd and what he thought about the authenticity of the videos that he purports to be Sasquatch. Stroud was more than candid and here is a portion of that interview.

Brian: "I've said it before and I'll say it again, and I've always done this, I do believe Todd Standing has had multiple encounters with Sasquatch. I just don't know about all the evidence presented. So, my question to you is, where are you on that with him? And what is your professional opinion? Let's just take the videos. For example, you're a filmmaker. So, you've looked at those... would you mind sharing your opinion on just the videos?"

Les Stroud: "Yeah, I've held the video hard drives in my hand, the hard drives downloaded from his cards in my hand and put them up in my edit suites. I know Todd's going to listen to this, so Todd, he knows how I feel about everything. I don't have an axe to grind and I also don't have any need to pander in one way or the other. With Todd. Sure. I've already said that Todd can be overly enthusiastic. Shall we say he's incredibly focused and driven in this subject matter.

"He has the focus and drive quite frankly, bordering on what you might consider to be autism or Asperger's syndrome. And I'm not saying that he has those. I'm saying that his drive and his focus is like that. It's very intent and very... 'it's gonna happen.' God love him for that.

"But that intensity turns off a lot of people. We look at individuals and go, 'I can't stand that guy; he's an asshole.' We say things like that about people with a strong intensity. I'm very judgmental. Don't get me wrong.

"I'm not saying any of this is true about Todd Standing, but I'm saying I don't judge people if they have a massive ego or if they're an asshole or whatever. Especially if they have something I want, because sometimes I'll be dealing with someone with a massive ego. But hey, he's the ticket in.

"So, when a personality like Todd's is there and he's doing any one of his talks or his videos, people get a vibe and many people don't like that vibe. All right. Fair enough. But regardless of whether you're not, you have a bad vibe. It's got nothing to do with whether or not he's telling the truth or presenting real evidence. Nothing whatsoever.

"So, I went out with him on several occasions, and what I can say about him to his credit. The man is boots on the ground. Absolutely. He will be out there for weeks on end again. There's that drive. There's that focus, right? So, he'll be out there for a week. So, if anybody is going to get something, he stands a good chance because he just doesn't quit.

"He's relentless by the same token. When we were out there, I called him many times. 'I don't think that's Bigfoot at all. I think that's an owl, right?' And to his credit, he would say, 'Yeah. You might be right." Now to somebody else. They might go, 'Oh, that's a Bigfoot.' And they might just buy into it.

"I never bought into anything. And when you're that way... he did respond in kind. He responded with, 'Okay you got a point.' But just saying the stuff that he presented to me at first, I looked at things and thought, 'Did Todd build this stick structure?'

"'Did he make these things?' And I'd say that right to him. Like I'm trying to think, but then I'm looking at it going, 'He's a strong dude, but not that strong,' kind of thing. So, you wanted me to speak more about the film, but before I get to the film, I had to premise my beliefs and my thoughts about Todd.

"So again, is everything that he presents real and accurate? I don't know. Haven't got a freaking clue, but I could say the same thing about Stacy Brown or David Paulides or Doug Hajicek. I don't know. Maybe Doug's story about the footprints in Quebec is a bunch of bullshit. I don't know. But I like to just say, but you know what, I'm going to believe you anyway, because life's too short not to.

"It's more fun to go. Yeah, this is cool. So, same thing with Todd. All right. So now we have this footage and maybe this is what you're referencing. I'm not sure what you're referencing about the footage, but I had it. I looked at it. I have some issues with it, and I've told him that 'I don't understand, Todd.'

"Why? 'We don't have all of the lead up footage. Where's all of the lead up footage of you scrambling and this happening' and then, he would say things to me as explain things to me as to why he doesn't and I'm not going to share that. That's for him to share. But I'm going to say that. I'm not so sure.

"I agreed with him and I told him I don't know, but anyway, that was a concern of mine. 'Where's all the lead up footage? All we ever see is that. I'm now working with you as a producer. I want everything leading to that.' And he didn't have it, right? So that I was very questionable. About what the Sasquatch look like.

"I get it. Big deal. Joe Rogan starts giggling and uncontrollably when he sees it... good on him. But look, man, I come from a very lower than-blue-collar background. I've sat in enough hockey arenas and dressing rooms, listening to a big ass buffoon jock who owns the room because he's laughing.

"'And if you don't laugh with me,' he's going to kick the crap out of you. I've been around that a lot. And so fine, you can get on there with different people who are just going to look at that imagery that Todd Standing has," and laugh their ass off, which gets everybody else laughing, which makes it like a high school thing, right?

"But I'm like you don't know. It's not... and I know guys like Thinker Thunker have gone into the film stuff, and every time I look at something online that claims to be able to debunk Todd Standing's footage, I can see the debunking in there debunking. I can see where they're saying... something that's not right.

"What you just said is wrong, and now you're basing everything that you're criticizing this footage on what you just said. And even though what you're saying might make sense, what you're basing it on doesn't make any sense. So, I've seen, I'm not going to get into detail, but I've seen that, in looking at stuff online.

"So here we are. Here's the crux of this though, and I think maybe this is what you're getting at. Here we are looking at these... I believe it's these two face images. One, everybody goes, oh, it looks like an Ewok. And then people try to say, oh, his wife worked as a special effects artist. She was a hairdresser, for crying out loud, and that she made these things up. And then there's the time lapse thing where you see Todd's face.

"Hey, that's all fun. Photoshop type work. Hey, have at it. You could probably do that with just about any photo. Probably do that with me and Patty, right? So, I don't buy into any of that. But what I can say is this... from my experience of knowing Todd Standing and seeing that footage and having it in my hands, I can't as a filmmaker say that it's fake.

"I can't as a person who knows Todd say that he's lying, and I would if I could. But I can't. And so, what are we left with... these two images? What is the problem everybody has with it? Here's my throwback to the crowd, of everybody in the community. As you say, the quote unquote community.

"It's this first of all. They don't really like him. Second of all, he shows us this footage. That third of all, if it's real, it's way better than Patty. And we love our Patty. We just have such an infatuation with Patty. Now we all want a better image, but here along comes Todd Standing with a personality that is difficult to manage and handle when you're listening to him speak.

"And he shows you this footage and your instinct is go, 'That's bullshit. That's made up. That's fake. Oh, that's all crap.' But everybody, including -- and I respect Thinker Thunker for the work he does -- but including Thinker Thunker in this situation, you don't know. And I don't agree with the little synopsis of how it's all fake because we don't know that it's fake.

"And if it's not fake, it's way better than Patty. It's a freaking frontal, facial, long-term video. In focus, right? So, this is what we're afraid of.

I don't know, I guess maybe if it had been David Paulides had presented those photographs. We either would have vilified David, or we would have accepted it because he's much more likable, shall I say. Or Jeff Meldrum.

"Okay, let's pick on Jeff. Jeff is like... you want him to be your dad. He's a wonderful human being. If it was Jeff's footage, we would have accepted it, but because Todd has this intensity to him... and that's where we're at, I think. I think that's where we're at.

"Todd reached out to me just recently to go on an expedition with him. I can't go cause I'm busy, I would, I'll tell you, I would. I would also say, I would be the same skeptic that I am and I've always been. And so should everybody that goes with him. He's very charismatic to some people, but also very problematic to others...maybe most. So, there you go. Did I touch on the points that you were thinking of, that I reached before? Did I miss something?"

I left that conversation with Les, even more perplexed and unsure of where I stood on Todd. Despite what Les felt about the footage, on that I was a bit more certain of it. I still felt that the videos were not authentic. The only person who could potentially sway my opinion was Todd Standing himself.

I had made several attempts to invite him onto the show. While he seemed receptive to the idea, it had yet to materialize. Interestingly, just a few weeks after my interview with Les Stroud aired, Todd agreed to appear on the show.

In mid-January 2022, Todd and I sat down for an interview. Todd was incredibly energetic and clearly passionate about the topic of Sasquatch. We immediately addressed the elephant in the room -- the fact that I had publicly labeled him a hoaxer -- and proceeded to discuss his research and the videos that I had previously dismissed as hoaxes. Here is an excerpt from that interview.

Brian: "I had a conversation with Les Stroud when Les was on the show. I talked about some of the evidence that you've put forward in some of the videos. I said to Les point blank, 'Todd Standing has the best HD quality evidence that Bigfoot exists on this planet that I've ever seen, or he's the greatest hoaxer that's ever lived.'

We had a conversation about that, that lasted about 30 minutes. At the end of that, Les was your biggest supporter in all of that. He was like, 'Look, I've spent time with this guy. He is the real deal. He is boots on the ground.'

"He said, 'As far as his video evidence is concerned,' he held those SD cards, the evidence, in his hand. And he said, he saw nothing in that video that or any of those videos that would lead him to believe that evidence is faked.

"I've said it on the show before that I thought that it's possible that stuff was faked, right? Now I've also talked to other people since I've talked to him. I interviewed Cameron Buckner last night for the show, and Cameron has met you and spent time with you and interviewed you. He said the exact same thing about you.

"So, I will be... I will be man enough to admit the shit I've said about you in the past. Let's talk a little bit about the videos, and the things that you've produced in the past, for those people that have those opinions. That stuff is an HD quality video of Sasquatch. What do you say to those people, like me in that camp, who had doubts about your footage?

Todd: "Gosh, look at the evidence that is against it! It's just ridiculously preposterous, right? You hear crap like, 'Because Jeff investigated at the very beginning, my dad dated a woman who owned a fabric store, so that proves them.' That's not true. 'My sister's a special effects major,' but that's not true. It's all lies.

"And what you hear from them is, 'Why are you proved him a fake?' but Jeff would go 'No, I need to hear it.' And they go, 'Why? His sister's a special effects artist.' She's not. And I proved that. I can prove that. But really, it's frustrating. Even some of the... probably the dumbest thing I hear.

"I'm sorry. It's ignorant. People put my head in the Sasquatch. And I just heard it last couple of days ago, 'So I can't get over the way your head matches up with the Sasquatch.' That's video five. It's Jake. And I did a video showing Jake's head... is... it's like this big, it's like that tall.

"And I conclusively proved it's... he's five times the size of my head and people are still 'all those proportions on that.' I don't know what to say. Like when people can't break the paradigm. What is profoundly in my defense is I take people out, and when Jeff Meldrum saw Sasquatch, he fricking well saw Sasquatch, man, like in three days with me.

"But wouldn't you expect that from a man who has eight videos public? Oh, 9, 10, 11, 12, all coming, my friend, more coming. I'm never going to stop. And what John talked about. John was with me for longer than Jeff. He did nine days straight with me. And John was like... he wouldn't even talk to me the first, I don't know, eight days.

"He was barely saying anything. He was so skeptical. He always had his arms crossed and he'd make funny faces. When he did that last day's interview, I was lucky I had it on a tripod. Cause I literally would have dropped the camera. Where he says, 'This is all real. This man's legit.' Like he did. He checked every backstory.

"This man was taking notes. He questioned me. Then he asked me specific details about every video, on and on, lists and lists of it. And all he found was absolute profound truth in every single thing, because it's not a story. I was there. You can ask me a question no one's ever asked me before, and I'll have you the answer that fast... because I just go, 'Oh yeah, that's what happened that day, or this is what was going on.'

"Cause it's all absolutely, 100 percent factual. And again, don't take my word for it. Come on, like *Survivorman*. That dude, when he came out with me, he said, 'Look. I'm going to get famous for proving you're a hoaxer and liar. Famous for proving that you're legit.'

"And what did he do? He's Survivorman. He's a beast. He's so freaking tough. And the stuff we did, backcountry, and he had so much faith in me. I was always his guide. I kept him safe. He was calm and never things like lost. Or he would literally go, 'Let's go there,' and we go that way.

"I go, 'Okay, what's over there is that, and this, there's some breaks over there. He's like, 'Dude, you've been everywhere.' 'I know,' I'm like, 'I know this whole area backwards and forwards.'...I know one one as good as the Sasquatch do. I'm legit out there. I legit fight for this discovery.

"There's a special effects makeup artist, that I spoke to from Wicca, who did like Lord of the Rings and stuff. He was gonna give me a job. He's like, Man, you're so amazing. It's clearly fake, but your stuff... you're incredible.' I'm like, 'I can't dude. I could never duplicate that,' but at the end of the conversation, he said, 'You know... what if you are faking this though? You're doing it to prove the species is real.'

"Ding ding! So, this is what you're left with. If I am faking it, I faked it for species protection, for species recognition, and to teach people about the species. Because I sure as shit am finding tracks. I sure as shit tell you that the structures and the breaks and the sightings... Like Jeff Meldrum will never ever. If you look at him and say, 'Oh, that was some dude; he had you tricked.' Jeff was there.

"Like you're in the hell of middle of nowhere. There's no dude smashing trees, busting the ground. Like Sasquatch came around, interacted, and then showed himself to Jeff. That's what makes Jeff so special too. Is people don't talk about that Sasquatch said, 'Look at this, bitch,' and he went right across that open area. And Jeff was standing right there.

"That Sasquatch was in 30 yards of him, and he let Jeff see him. That year I left, teary eyed, because they just showed themselves to a PhD,

Jeff Meldrum. How brave were they? If Jeff would have had a gun, he would have blown holes in them. But they'd been watching Jeff for three days. And Jeff has been obsessed with this topic his whole life since he was a little nerdy boy.

"And that's why they did that. Because they know. They know; they get it. We're just going to keep making this discovery happen. I am... I'm so proud of the footage I have. I don't do expeditions so much like that anymore. Cause it was nearly killing me. Like I would nearly... I would... I'd come back from those expeditions and just lay down for three days and just get fed, sleep, and recover.

"I would lose -- I'm lean -- and I'd lose 20, 30 pounds of muscle. Like it was like Navy SEAL training. I'd go there and just annihilate my body. And I would fail most times. One in 10 times, I'd get success, and all the effort and all the blood that I put into it... and see nobody questions that anymore.

"Anybody who's been out with me, they know my skillset. They know I'm an excellent tracker. I had a Ranger, the special forces Ranger dude, come up. They dropped his knife. He's like, 'Oh my God, I'll never find it.' I'm like, 'Dude, I'll backtrack'. He goes, 'Are you really that good?' Two hours later, boom, there's his knife.

"Backtracked right to the spot. So, you 'get it' when you come out with me. That's why Jeff and Les have so much faith. Cause they've been out with me. They bled. Jeff Meldrum is a tough dude. When I took him out those years ago, man he never missed a step. He's one tough, awesome, amazing dude.

"And it goes back to them, to Survivorman's a freaking beast. He's the godfather of survival TV. That guy is so tough. I couldn't do what he does. You wanna hear me say something? I couldn't do 10 days. If you did 10 days in the bush with me with no food, either I would die, or the bear that tried to kill me would die. Somebody's gonna die.

"He's got that endurance body. Wait, like I'm 6'3 he's 5'10. I'm 220 he's like 180. And those little guys will kill ya in the endurance. People talk about The Rock and all these big dudes. Those little guys will smoke you every time, they've got endurance for miles.

"If you're one of those little dudes and you're tough... sprinters get killed, and this is a long race. Everything you do is about the length of time, and those guys are endurance monsters like Survivorman. I just, I have so much respect for him.

"He asked me to do *Survivorman*. I was like, I can't do that. You're a freaking animal, man. There's no way survival. 'Let's just start you on in seven days. Seven days, no food.' Nope. That takes years off your life because I used to do that crap. But I'm not built for that anymore. I'm wiser.

"Now, when the stuff comes out about the success = they're taking apples now for me, they're making little cool structures for me, they're interacting with my expeditioners that are coming back over and over... I literally have a full time Sasquatch research center in Canada, in the hottest spot I've ever found in the world. Where the Sasquatch are interacting with people, and I'm in every second week and someone else is in every second week.

"And something's gonna break because it's just... it's too much. Absolutely astonishing, amazing things happening for this research. Be excited, get excited. Don't lose hope. Don't lose faith, and... even talking about my footage too. I met... I met Bob Gimlin. You know *everybody* called his footage fake in the beginning, and it did the test of time.

'That's what you're doing... the test of time,' I remember he told me once. He stood up on a table and talked to people at the Sasquatch summit 20 years ago. 'I was this man. I saw a Sasquatch,' he held up a picture of Jake. 'And this is a Sasquatch.' He said, 20 years ago, 'Todd, they'll be giving you little awards and stuff like this. But I remember how you [the audience] treated me for 20 years. I was a liar and a fraud, just like you're doing to this man right here.'

"History is repeating itself. And that's why you're coming around. That's why everybody's going to come around because I'm not going anywhere. And I am telling the truth, and the truth will set me free. And I am going to be transparent because it's made me a very happy person."

After my interview with Todd, I gained a newfound respect for his research. While it didn't change my belief that he had hoaxed the videos, I felt I had a better understanding of his motivations.

About a year after my interview with Todd, I met a young podcaster and Sasquatch researcher named Kyle Dechene. Kyle had encountered what he believed to be a Sasquatch in the Adirondacks with his father, Richard, which led to a meeting with Todd Standing. Todd had flown out to investigate their encounter site and thus began a friendship between Kyle and Todd.

Kyle made several trips to Radium for research and started the *Discovering Bigfoot* podcast, which was broadcast weekly on Todd's *Sylvanic Bigfoot* [YouTube channel]. He interviewed eyewitnesses and defended Todd, his videos, and his research. I invited Kyle on my show to discuss his experience with his dad, and his Sasquatch sighting, during an expedition with Todd at his Radium research area.

Over the next year, Kyle and I guested on each other's podcasts, and he consistently encouraged me to join an expedition in Canada. Despite my interest, my show production schedule, speaking events, and writing this book didn't allow for a week-long trip into British Columbia's backcountry.

However, a lingering doubt remained. Could I be wrong about Todd? I had accused him of hoaxing his videos and questioned the authenticity of the experiences of those who had been on expeditions with him. The only way to truly get closer to the truth about Todd was to visit his research site, spend time with him, and test my hypothesis.

In the early summer of 2023, I committed to making the week-long trip in October. I flew out of Charlotte, North Carolina, on October 2nd, and Richard flew in from New York. We met Kyle in Calgary, who had flown in from Florida a few days earlier and spent some time at base camp alone. We drove to Todd's house to meet him and Ashley, his girlfriend and research partner.

Jason Schute arrived shortly before we were leaving. He was planning a solo trek to the top of Radium for a ten-day odyssey into the wilderness. However, the airline had lost his luggage, leaving him with only the clothes on his back. He planned to stay the night at Todd's and wait to see if his bag could be located, which would determine his next steps.

With our meals secured, Kyle, Richard, and I hopped back into the truck to head off to the store to purchase the rest of our supplies for the week. Once we were done, we hit the road for the three-hour journey from Calgary to our base camp. After exiting the highway, we veered onto a logging road. I asked Kyle how much further we had left to go before we got to base camp, and he said that we had another twenty-eight kilometers, or just over seventeen miles, to cover on these logging roads.

Merriam-Webster describes "remote" as being separated by a space or interval greater than usual, far removed in space, time, or relation. I can now personally attest that driving seventeen miles deep into the forest gives a whole new perspective to the term "remote."

A few miles short of our base camp, we stopped to refill our water bottles from the river. I was astounded by the pristine beauty of the surroundings and the crystal-clear, rapidly flowing glacial water. Kyle decided to do some ice bathing, while Richard and I focused on filling our bottles.

We had previously discussed ice bathing, a practice that Todd, Kyle, and Ashley had integrated into their Sasquatch research. Ice bathing, also known as cold water immersion or cryotherapy, is a recovery method where one submerges one's body in cold water for a specific duration. This is typically done in a tub filled with ice and water, with temperatures usually between 50 to 59 degrees Fahrenheit (10 to 15 degrees Celsius).

Ice bathing is thought to alleviate muscle soreness and inflammation following strenuous physical activity. The cold temperature can constrict blood vessels and decrease metabolic activity, reducing swelling and tissue breakdown. The cold water can help flush out toxins and lactic acid accumulated in the muscles, while also promoting the flow of oxygen-rich blood, aiding recovery. Some research suggests that regular exposure to cold water can enhance the immune system by increasing white blood cell circulation. Cold water immersion can stimulate endorphin production, the body's natural painkillers and mood boosters.

The body has to exert more effort to maintain its core temperature in cold water, potentially increasing metabolic rate and aiding weight loss. Some people find that ice bathing can improve their sleep, possibly due to the physical cooling of the body and the reduction in muscle soreness. It's crucial to note that while many people vouch for the benefits of ice bathing, scientific research on its effectiveness is still ongoing and results are inconclusive.

Kyle fully submerged himself from the waist down, while Richard and I waded in up to our knees. If you've never experienced submerging any part of your body in freezing cold water, it's a sensation that's hard to describe. Initially, my feet and legs felt cold. Then came the numbness, and after about a minute, I couldn't feel much at all. That was my signal to get out. My feet and legs started to burn as I dried them off, but honestly, they felt fantastic once that subsided. Throughout the week, I repeated this process a few times with my hands and lower arms.

Leaving the river behind, we continued our slow drive towards our base camp for the week. Nestled amidst the thick forest, the camp consisted of nothing more than two modest campers positioned in a small clearing. With our supplies unloaded, we eagerly set off on our first of many exhilarating hikes.

During our drive to the camp, Kyle pointed out countless broken trees, scattered alongside the old logging road. Over the course of the week, I would take many photos and videos of these intriguing tree breaks.

Guiding us through the area, Kyle pointed out several alleged Sasquatch footprints that he, Todd, and others had discovered in the research area. The forest's sphagnum moss proved to be an exceptional medium, preserving these prints with remarkable clarity. Some of these purported Sasquatch prints were said to be over five years old, yet they were almost perfectly preserved in the spongy ground. While a few of these prints were certainly compelling, I couldn't definitively conclude whether they were the impressions of a Sasquatch or not.

The same was true when it came to the tree breaks, we encountered, leaving me pondering whether they were caused by a natural occurrence such as snow load, or if they could be some cryptic symbol left behind by a nine-foot-tall bipedal hominid. Either way, it was looking as though my weeklong expedition may leave me with more questions than answers.

We returned to our campsite, and Kyle to the business of warming up our dinner. Todd and Ashley were staying at Todd's place with Jason and wouldn't be joining us until the next day. Kyle, Richard, and I gathered around the campfire, eating our meals and eagerly anticipating the adventures that the next six days might bring. We were all worn out from the day's journey, so we decided to turn in early. I was too tired to set up my audio recorders, so I didn't capture any sounds that first night.

The next morning, I woke up around eight and headed over to Kyle and Richard's camper to brew some coffee. It was a team effort, as I had the coffee, and they had the French press -- one was useless without the other. With no cell service, we couldn't contact Todd, Jason, or Ashley, so we decided to visit a nearby scenic overlook and waterfall. After breakfast, we packed up the truck and set off to explore, but we ran into Jason on the logging road not far from our camp.

We turned around and followed him back to meet up and formulate a new game plan. The airline hadn't found his bag, but Jason didn't want to waste any more time. He bought a new 65-liter backpack and all-new gear for his ten-day solo trek up Radium Mountain and deep into the wilderness.

We spent the next hour helping Jason pack his new bag with the supplies he'd need to withstand the chilly nighttime temperatures, which were already in the mid-thirties. He would likely face temperatures fifteen degrees colder once he reached the mountain's summit during the first part of his journey. Once his supplies were packed, we all climbed back into the truck to drive to the mountain's base, with Jason leading the way in another vehicle. We decided to postpone the hike we had planned for another day. Today, we would accompany Jason for a significant part of his ascent up the mountain.

The mountainous landscape was breathtakingly gorgeous, and the hike was nothing short of spectacular. However, this was far from a leisurely walk on a level trail. It was evident from the get-go that this was not a hike for novices. The majority of the narrow path was a steep incline, with some sections having a seven to ten percent gradient. There were moments when we had to use our hands to keep our balance and navigate the challenging terrain.

As we ascended, my admiration for Jason grew. I was carrying a small backpack with a water bottle and some snacks, and I was feeling the burn in my legs and glutes. Jason, on the other hand, was carrying a full pack that I estimated to weigh between ninety and one hundred pounds. To say that Jason is a beast would be an understatement.

About two-thirds of the way through our journey, we found a picturesque spot by the river to stop for lunch and refill our water bottles. After finishing our sandwiches and rehydrating, we resumed our hike. Progress was slow, with Jason hiking for five minutes and resting for ten. That was the nature of this hike. Eventually, we reached the part of the river where Jason would cross to continue his ascent, and we would go our separate ways. I managed to capture some fantastic footage of Jason as he crossed the river and began his zigzagging journey to the peak. You can view these photos and videos in the interactive section of this book.

After saying our goodbyes to Jason, Kyle, Richard, and I began our descent. I can assure you; that the journey down was much easier than the climb up.

Back at base camp, we lit a fire and Kyle once again prepared our dinner. If you've never had a meal in the heart of the forest, by an open fire, you're truly missing out. I must admit, food really does taste better outdoors. As the sun disappeared behind the trees, we started hearing some peculiar sounds that I still can't explain. We all heard what sounded like wood knocking and some odd whoops. The wood knocking sounded more like a massive rock being hit against a tree about 200 yards away. We only heard it a few times, but it was reminiscent of a sound I had only heard once before.

During the summer of 2023, on our property in North Carolina, I had heard what seemed like four powerful knocks. I had stepped out onto our deck around three in the morning and heard the knocks coming from the ridge to the north of us, about a quarter mile away. I had never heard anything like it before or since. That is, until I found myself in the middle of nowhere in BC, Canada, some twenty-four hundred miles away.

Todd and Ashley joined us the next day and we began our exploration of the expansive wilderness on foot. We spent each day hiking for at least six hours. We found tree breaks, peculiar structures, and what seemed to be footprints. During one hike in an area dense with large tree structures, I stumbled upon what appeared to be a trackway left in the moss. I was able to follow it and identify at least eight steps. It was one of the most remarkable discoveries of our expedition. I can't confirm that it was a Sasquatch trackway, but it certainly made me consider the possibility.

Honestly, the amount of potential evidence of Sasquatch activity in that area was staggering. After observing so many tree breaks, structures, and potential footprints, I found myself questioning what else it could be? I considered every possibility for each new discovery. Could it be a bear? A human? A wolf? Each time, the answer was no, leading me back to the possibility of Sasquatch.

That evening, Todd and Ashley chose to camp a few miles away while Kyle, Richard, and I maintained our usual routine at base camp. To be honest, I was slightly apprehensive about them separating from the group. I had entered the expedition with a high degree of skepticism, expecting some sort of hoax. If that was the plan, then tonight seemed like the perfect opportunity.

As dusk fell, similar to previous nights, we heard what sounded like tree knocks and a peculiar vocalization. Both sounds originated from the opposite direction of Todd and Ashley's camp. Luckily, I had spent two and a half days familiarizing myself with the area, so I knew that Todd and Ashley wouldn't have had time to reach their camp, let alone time to run through the woods to create the sounds we heard.

Just like previous nights, the activity ceased as abruptly as it started. However, unlike previous nights, the sky was clear, and the stars were out in full force. We found ourselves gazing upwards as we warmed ourselves by the fire. I think I was the first to notice something unusual in the night sky.

I saw a bright sphere of light moving at a high speed from left to right. We had seen a few commercial planes flying from Alberta to Calgary, but this object was much larger and higher in the sky. We estimated it to be around 80,000 feet up, moving at several thousand miles per hour. Kyle and Richard joined me in tracking the object, and soon we spotted more. At one point, we were tracking up to ten objects. We rushed to grab our binoculars for a closer look.

Through my binoculars, I saw a bright blue light, but no discernible details. As I watched it ascend, it suddenly stopped and made a sharp left turn before speeding off. At that moment, I knew we were witnessing something extraordinary, possibly extraterrestrial.

We continued to observe the sky for the next hour, during which we saw a meteor explode overhead and at least six shooting stars. It was one of the most incredible nights of stargazing I've ever experienced. As the fire began to die down and fatigue set in from our day of hiking, we decided to call it a night.

That was the only night we observed strange phenomena in the sky, but the odd knocks and other unusual sounds near base camp persisted throughout the week. Todd and Ashley reported a daytime encounter with two Sasquatches near a large tree structure. Richard saw a large shadow lurking nearby while he was relieving himself in the early morning hours. Once daylight broke, Kyle, Richard, and I investigated the area and found two large impressions in the moss resembling footprints.

Although the narratives of encounters are intriguing, they don't provide the irrefutable evidence I require for personal conviction. My time in British Columbia was riddled with inexplicable occurrences. Damaged trees, peculiar tree formations, and possible footprints are all fascinating, but I need to witness one of these beings firsthand. Sadly, I left Canada with more questions than answers.

Upon returning from my Sasquatch expedition with Standing, I was met with an unexpected wave of hostility from the Sasquatch community. The expedition had been an exciting adventure, filled with the thrill of the unknown and the hope of encountering the elusive creature. However, the community's reaction was far from what I had anticipated.

Some individuals in the Sasquatch community were outraged at my decision to collaborate with Todd Standing. Standing, a controversial figure within the community, is widely regarded as a hoaxer. His reputation for fabricating evidence and staging encounters with the Sasquatch has earned him the ire of many enthusiasts and researchers.

The community accused me of giving a platform to a known hoaxer, thereby undermining the credibility of genuine Sasquatch research. They argued that by associating with Standing, I was indirectly endorsing his deceptive practices. The backlash was intense, with many members expressing their disappointment and anger on various online forums and social media platforms.

The situation was further exacerbated when I discovered a YouTube video created by a group of content creators who had also embarked on an expedition with Standing. In the video, they revealed that they had found fake gorilla gloves in Standing's vehicle during their trip. This discovery raised serious questions about the authenticity of Standing's claims and his credibility as a Sasquatch researcher.

When confronted about the gloves, Standing claimed that they were a joke gift from his brother-in-law. However, this explanation did little to quell the growing skepticism and mistrust within the community. Many saw it as a weak attempt to cover up his fraudulent activities.

The revelation of the gorilla gloves, coupled with the community's vehement disapproval, cast a dark shadow over my expedition with Standing. What had initially been an exciting adventure had turned into a source of controversy and conflict. Despite the backlash, I remain committed to my pursuit of understanding the Sasquatch, albeit with a newfound awareness of the complexities and controversies that surround this elusive creature.

Here is a group of photos of potential footprints taken during my
Radium BC expedition in the fall of 2023.

Here is a photo of Kyle and his dad, Richard Dechene, helping Jason
across the river before starting his ascent.

Here is my friend and guide, Kyle Dechene (5'8"), providing some scale
to show the height of a tree break.

7

THE PERILS OF PERCEPTION: PAREIDOLIA AND MISIDENTIFICATION

The search for Sasquatch is fraught with challenges. Beyond those instances that we have identified as hoaxes, there are two significant obstacles that further complicate this endeavor: pareidolia and misidentification.

In this chapter, we explore the intricate details of these phenomena and their impact on Sasquatch research. By understanding the complexities of perception and the potential for misinterpretation, we can navigate the blurred lines between genuine evidence and mere illusions.

Pareidolia: The Power of Pattern Recognition

Pareidolia is a psychological phenomenon that involves perceiving meaningful patterns or images where none exist. Our brains are wired to recognize patterns, faces, and familiar shapes, even in random or ambiguous stimuli. In the context of Sasquatch research, pareidolia can lead individuals to interpret natural formations, shadows, or foliage as evidence of the creature's presence. This tendency to see what we expect or desire to see can cloud objectivity and contribute to false positives in the search for Sasquatch. This psychological phenomenon has played a significant role in the world of Sasquatch research, making it a daunting task to separate fact from fiction and weed through the nonsense to uncover genuine evidence of Sasquatch's existence.

Pareidolia is a natural mechanism deeply ingrained in the human brain. From an evolutionary standpoint, it served as a survival advantage, allowing our ancestors to quickly identify potential threats or opportunities in their environment. However, in the context of Sasquatch research, this innate tendency can lead to misinterpretations and false sightings.

Imagine a dense forest, shrouded in mist, with towering trees and tangled undergrowth. As Sasquatch researchers venture into this wilderness, their senses become heightened, their minds primed to detect any signs of the elusive creature. Every rustle of leaves, every shadowy figure, and every twisted tree trunk becomes a potential clue, a potential sighting of the legendary Sasquatch.

In this heightened state of anticipation, the human mind seeks patterns and familiar shapes, even in the absence of concrete evidence. A cluster of rocks may resemble a face, a fallen tree branch may mimic an arm, and a patch of foliage may take on the form of a hulking figure. The researchers, driven by their passion and desire to find evidence, may inadvertently attribute these ambiguous stimuli to the presence of the Sasquatch.

This is where pareidolia takes hold, blurring the line between reality and imagination. The mind, eager to make sense of the world, fills in the gaps and creates connections that may not truly exist. It is a subconscious process, driven by our innate need for meaning and understanding. The researchers, caught in the grip of pareidolia, may genuinely believe they have encountered the Sasquatch, only to realize later that their perception was influenced by this psychological phenomenon.

In addition to what people report seeing, many encounters include hearing strange noises while out in remote areas throughout North America. These purported vocalizations, howls, and whoops are certainly not immune to misinterpretation. Auditory pareidolia is a psychological phenomenon where the brain interprets random or ambiguous sounds as being significant or meaningful, often in the form of recognizable words, phrases, or even music. This phenomenon is a subset of pareidolia, which is the tendency of human beings to perceive familiar patterns or forms where none exist. Pareidolia can also manifest visually, such as seeing faces in clouds or religious figures in toast.

The term "pareidolia" comes from the Greek words *para*, meaning "beside" or "alongside," and *eidolon*, meaning "image" or "form." It was first used in the 19th century to describe the human tendency to impose familiar patterns on random stimuli. Auditory pareidolia specifically refers to the perception of meaningful sounds in noise.

The human brain is a pattern-seeking machine, constantly looking for familiar structures in the environment. This is a survival mechanism, as recognizing patterns allows us to predict and respond to our surroundings effectively. However, this tendency can sometimes lead us astray, causing us to perceive patterns where none exist. This is the case with auditory pareidolia.

Auditory pareidolia can occur with any type of sound, but it is particularly common with ambiguous or complex sounds, such as white noise, nature sounds, or even the hum of a refrigerator. The brain tries to make sense of these sounds by matching them to familiar patterns, often resulting in the perception of words or music.

This phenomenon may play a significant role in many reported encounters with Sasquatch. Individuals who believe they have heard the calls or vocalizations of a Sasquatch are often experiencing auditory pareidolia. The sounds they hear – rustling leaves, animal calls, or the wind blowing through trees – are interpreted by their brains as the distinctive calls of this elusive creature.

The role of expectation and belief cannot be understated in these instances. If an individual is in a forested area known for Sasquatch sightings and is actively listening for signs of the creature, they are more likely to interpret ambiguous sounds as Sasquatch calls. This is due to a cognitive bias known as "confirmation bias," where people tend to interpret information in a way that confirms their pre-existing beliefs.

In many cases, these sounds are later analyzed by experts and found to be the calls of known animals, such as owls, coyotes, or even humans. However, for the individuals who heard them, the experience of hearing a Sasquatch was very real. This is a testament to the power of auditory pareidolia and the human brain's remarkable ability to find patterns in noise.

Auditory pareidolia is a fascinating phenomenon that highlights the brain's pattern-seeking nature and the influence of expectation and belief on perception. While it may lead some to believe they have heard the calls of a Sasquatch, it also provides a rational explanation for these experiences.

The challenge lies in distinguishing genuine evidence from mere illusions. The Bigfoot research community is inundated with countless photographs, videos, and eyewitness testimonies, each claiming to capture the elusive creature. However, the majority of these pieces of evidence are tainted by pareidolia, making it difficult to separate the wheat from the chaff.

To overcome this obstacle, researchers must approach their investigations with a critical eye and a healthy dose of skepticism. They must be aware of the potential influence of pareidolia and strive to eliminate bias from their analysis. This requires a rigorous examination of the evidence, seeking corroborating accounts, and employing scientific methodologies to ensure objectivity.

In the quest for the truth about Sasquatch, it is crucial to acknowledge the role of pareidolia and its impact on Sasquatch research. By understanding this phenomenon, researchers can navigate through the sea of ambiguous stimuli and false sightings, gradually uncovering the genuine evidence that may finally shed light on the existence of the legendary creature. It is a challenging endeavor, but one that holds the promise of unraveling one of the greatest mysteries of our time.

Eyewitness misidentification is another significant challenge in Sasquatch research. Eyewitness testimony has long been considered a valuable source of information in various fields, including Sasquatch research.

Human perception is subjective and prone to errors, especially in high-stress or unfamiliar situations. When encountering an unknown or unexpected creature in the wilderness, witnesses may rely on memory, which can be influenced by biases, cultural expectations, and the power of suggestion. This can lead to misidentifications, where mundane animals, humans, or even inanimate objects are mistakenly perceived as Sasquatch.

Factors Contributing to Misidentification

Several factors contribute to misidentification in Sasquatch research. First, the fleeting nature of sightings and the often, limited visibility make it challenging to gather accurate information. Witnesses may only catch a glimpse of a large, bipedal figure in the distance, leaving room for interpretation and misjudgment. Additionally, the lack of familiarity with local wildlife or the presence of rare or unusual animals can further confuse witnesses, leading them to attribute their encounter to Sasquatch.

Cultural Influences and Expectations

Cultural influences and preconceived expectations also play a significant role in misidentification. The pervasive presence of Sasquatch in popular culture, folklore, and media can shape people's perceptions and predispose them to interpret their encounters as Sasquatch sightings. The power of suggestion, combined with the desire for validation and the need to fit within the cultural narrative, can lead witnesses to misidentify mundane phenomena as evidence of these creatures.

Cultural influences and expectations play a significant role in shaping our perceptions, beliefs, and interpretations of the world around us. This is particularly true in the realm of cryptozoology. The cultural context in which a person operates can significantly influence their approach to Sasquatch research and their interpretation of potential encounters.

Cultural influences can be seen in the way different societies perceive and interpret the existence of Sasquatch. For instance, in Native American cultures, Sasquatch is often considered a spiritual being or a part of their ancestral folklore. This cultural belief can influence a researcher from this background to approach Sasquatch research with a sense of reverence and respect, viewing it as a quest to understand a sacred entity rather than merely proving the existence of an elusive creature.

On the other hand, in Western cultures, Sasquatch is often viewed with skepticism and is associated with hoaxes and tall tales. A researcher from this cultural background may approach Sasquatch research with a more scientific and skeptical mindset, seeking concrete evidence to validate or debunk the existence of Sasquatch.

Cultural expectations also play a significant role in shaping a person's interpretation of a potential Sasquatch encounter. For instance, if a person has been raised in a culture where Sasquatch is considered a myth or a hoax, they may be more likely to dismiss an unusual encounter in the woods as a misidentification of a known animal or a trick of the light. They may also feel social pressure to keep their experience to themselves for fear of ridicule or disbelief.

Conversely, in a culture where belief in Sasquatch is more accepted or even expected, a person may be more likely to interpret an ambiguous encounter as a Sasquatch sighting. They may feel validated and supported in sharing their experience, and their account may be more readily accepted by their community.

Cultural influences and expectations can also shape the methodologies and tools a researcher uses in their Sasquatch research. For instance, a researcher from a Western scientific background may rely heavily on physical evidence such as footprints, hair samples, or photographic evidence. In contrast, a researcher from a Native American background may place more emphasis on oral histories, spiritual experiences, and personal encounters.

Cultural influences and expectations significantly shape a person's approach to Sasquatch research and their interpretation of potential encounters. They can influence the researcher's mindset, methodology, and the way they interpret and share their experiences. Understanding these cultural influences can provide valuable insights into the diverse perspectives and approaches in the field of Sasquatch research.

Memory and Recall

Human memory is not a flawless recording device but rather a reconstructive process influenced by various factors. Eyewitnesses often rely on memory to recount their Sasquatch encounters, but memory is susceptible to distortion, forgetting, and reconstruction.

Human memory and recall are complex cognitive processes that play a significant role in our daily lives. They allow us to store, retain, and retrieve information about our experiences, knowledge, and skills. However, memory is not a perfect recording of events. It is susceptible to various influences and can be distorted or altered over time. This chapter will explore how human memory and recall work, what can affect them, and how they play a factor in individuals who claim to have an encounter with a Sasquatch.

Memory is often divided into three stages: encoding, storage, and retrieval. Encoding is the process of converting sensory input into a form that can be stored in the brain. Storage involves maintaining the encoded information over time. Retrieval is the process of accessing and bringing the stored information into consciousness.

Several factors can affect memory and recall. Stress and trauma can significantly impact memory encoding and retrieval. High-stress situations can lead to heightened memory of certain details but can also result in memory gaps or distortions. Fatigue, alcohol, and drugs can also impair memory function.

The passage of time can lead to memory decay, where details of an event become less clear. Additionally, our memories can be influenced by subsequent information or experiences, a phenomenon known as retroactive interference. For instance, hearing others' accounts of an event can alter our own memory of that event.

Memory and recall play a significant role in Sasquatch encounters. When a person claims to have seen a Sasquatch, they are relying on their memory of the event. However, the factors mentioned above can influence the accuracy of this memory.

For instance, a Sasquatch sighting is likely to be a high-stress situation, which could impact the person's memory encoding and retrieval. They may vividly remember certain details, such as the creature's size or the fear they felt, but other details may be hazy or distorted.

The passage of time can also affect the person's memory of the encounter. As time goes on, their memory may decay, and details may become less clear. They may also be influenced by subsequent information, such as other people's Sasquatch sightings or media portrayals of Sasquatch. This can lead to retroactive interference, where their original memory is altered by this new information.

Human memory and recall are complex and fallible processes that can be influenced by various factors. These factors can impact the accuracy of a person's memory of a Sasquatch encounter. Therefore, while personal accounts of Sasquatch sightings are valuable, they should be considered with an understanding of the complexities and potential inaccuracies of human memory.

Perception and Interpretation

Perception is subjective, and individuals may interpret sensory information differently based on their biases, expectations, and prior experiences. In Sasquatch sightings, witnesses may perceive ambiguous stimuli, such as shadows, sounds, or fleeting glimpses, and interpret them as evidence of the creature.

Perception and interpretation are fundamental cognitive processes that allow us to make sense of the world around us. Perception refers to the process of receiving, selecting, organizing, and interpreting sensory information. Interpretation, on the other hand, involves assigning meaning to the perceived information based on our past experiences, knowledge, beliefs, and cultural background.

Perception begins with sensory input. Our senses (sight, hearing, touch, smell, and taste) receive stimuli from the environment, which are then converted into neural signals and sent to the brain. The brain organizes this sensory information into a coherent representation of the world. This process is influenced by several factors, including the intensity and quality of the stimuli, our physiological state (e.g., fatigue, hunger), and our attentional focus.

Interpretation involves assigning meaning to the perceived information. This process is heavily influenced by our past experiences, knowledge, beliefs, and cultural background. For instance, if we see a shape in the woods that resembles a human figure, our brain might interpret it as a person based on our past experiences and knowledge. However, if we believe in the existence of Sasquatch and are in an area where Sasquatch sightings have been reported, we might interpret the same shape as a Sasquatch.

Perception and interpretation play a significant role in Sasquatch encounters. When a person claims to have seen a Sasquatch, they are interpreting sensory information based on their perceptual processes and cognitive biases. Several factors can influence this process.

Firstly, the quality of the sensory input can affect perception. For instance, a sighting in low light conditions or at a great distance can lead to ambiguous or incomplete sensory information, making it more susceptible to misinterpretation.

Secondly, cognitive biases can influence interpretation. Confirmation bias, for instance, can lead a person to interpret ambiguous information in a way that confirms their pre-existing beliefs. If a person already believes in the existence of Sasquatch, they may be more likely to interpret ambiguous sensory information (e.g., a large, shadowy figure in the woods) as a Sasquatch.

Cultural influences can also shape interpretation. As discussed in previous chapters, in cultures where belief in Sasquatch is prevalent, individuals may be more likely to interpret ambiguous encounters as Sasquatch sightings.

Lastly, the influence of others can shape perception and interpretation. Social pressure or the desire to belong can lead individuals to interpret their experiences in line with group beliefs. For instance, if a person is part of a group that believes in Sasquatch, they may be more likely to interpret an ambiguous encounter as a Sasquatch sighting.

Perception and interpretation are complex processes influenced by a multitude of factors. These factors can significantly shape a person's interpretation of a potential Sasquatch encounter. Understanding these processes can provide valuable insights into the experiences of individuals who claim to have seen a Sasquatch and highlight the need for careful consideration of these factors in Sasquatch research.

Attention and Focus

During a Sasquatch sighting, witnesses may experience heightened emotions, fear, or excitement, which can impact their attention and focus. In such situations, individuals may selectively attend to certain details while disregarding others. This selective attention can result in incomplete or distorted recollections, as witnesses may fail to notice crucial aspects of the encounter or misremember details due to their emotional state.

Attention and focus are fundamental cognitive processes that allow us to selectively concentrate on a specific aspect of our environment while ignoring other perceivable information. These processes are crucial for our ability to interact with the world around us and play a significant role in shaping our experiences, including alleged encounters with creatures like Sasquatch.

Attention can be broadly categorized into two types: selective attention and divided attention. Selective attention refers to the ability to focus on a specific stimulus while ignoring irrelevant stimuli. For instance, when you are reading a book in a noisy café, your selective attention allows you to concentrate on the words in the book while ignoring the background noise. Divided attention, on the other hand, involves the ability to pay attention to multiple stimuli at the same time, such as driving while talking to a passenger.

Several factors can influence our attention and focus. These include the intensity and novelty of the stimulus, our physiological state (e.g., fatigue, hunger), our emotional state (e.g., stress, excitement), and our interests and goals. For instance, a loud noise or a brightly colored object is more likely to grab our attention due to its intensity and novelty. Similarly, if we are tired or hungry, our ability to focus can be impaired. Our emotional state can also influence our attention; for example, we are more likely to notice stimuli that are relevant to our current emotional state. Lastly, our interests and goals can guide our attention. If we are interested in birds, for instance, we are more likely to notice a bird in a tree than someone with no interest in birds.

Attention and focus play a significant role in alleged Sasquatch encounters. When a person is in an environment where a Sasquatch sighting is possible, their attention and focus are likely to be influenced by their interest in and belief about Sasquatch. If they believe in the existence of Sasquatch and are actively looking for it, they are more likely to pay attention to stimuli that might indicate the presence of Sasquatch, such as unusual sounds or movements in the woods.

But this heightened focus can also lead to misinterpretations. In the context of Sasquatch encounters, a person with a strong belief in Sasquatch might misinterpret an ambiguous stimulus (e.g., a shadowy figure in the woods) as a Sasquatch due to their heightened focus and expectation.

Additionally, the person's physiological and emotional state can also influence their attention and interpretation. For instance, if a person is tired or scared, their attention might be more focused on potential threats, making them more likely to misinterpret ambiguous stimuli as a Sasquatch.

Attention and focus are complex cognitive processes that are influenced by various factors. These factors can significantly shape a person's experience and interpretation of a potential Sasquatch encounter. Understanding these processes can provide valuable insights into the experiences of individuals who claim to have seen a Sasquatch and highlight the need for careful consideration of these factors in Sasquatch research.

Suggestibility

Eyewitnesses can be susceptible to suggestion and confirmation bias, where they unconsciously seek information that confirms their preexisting beliefs or expectations. In Sasquatch sightings, witnesses may be influenced by the prevailing cultural narrative, media portrayals, or the desire to fit within the Bigfoot community. This bias can lead witnesses to interpret their experiences in a way that aligns with their preconceived notions, potentially distorting their recollections and compromising the reliability of their testimony.

Suggestibility is a psychological concept that refers to the degree to which an individual's perceptions, memories, and actions can be influenced by external factors such as suggestions, ideas, or information from others. It is a common phenomenon in human cognition and behavior, and it plays a significant role in various aspects of our lives, including our beliefs, attitudes, and memories.

Suggestibility can significantly influence individuals who believe they have had an encounter with a Sasquatch, also known as Bigfoot. This is because our perceptions and memories are not always accurate representations of reality. They can be easily distorted or influenced by various factors, including our expectations, beliefs, emotions, and the information we receive from others.

For instance, if an individual has a strong belief in the existence of Sasquatch and is exposed to suggestive information or ideas about Sasquatch, such as stories, images, or alleged evidence, they may be more likely to interpret ambiguous experiences or stimuli (e.g., unidentified sounds or footprints in the woods) as encounters with Sasquatch. This is known as confirmation bias, a type of cognitive bias that leads us to favor information that confirms our preexisting beliefs or hypotheses.

Moreover, if an individual has a vivid imagination or is highly susceptible to suggestions, they may be more likely to form false memories of encountering Sasquatch, especially if they are encouraged or pressured to recall such experiences by others. This is known as memory suggestibility, a phenomenon where our memories can be altered or fabricated by suggestive information or techniques.

Suggestibility in humans can be influenced by various factors. One of the most significant factors is individual differences in personality and cognitive style. For example, individuals who are more imaginative, compliant, or anxious, or who have a lower cognitive ability, are generally more suggestible.

Social factors can also influence suggestibility. For instance, authoritative or persuasive individuals, such as leaders, experts, or charismatic figures, can exert a strong influence on our beliefs and memories. Similarly, social pressure or conformity can increase suggestibility, as we tend to align our beliefs and memories with those of the majority of the group we belong to.

The context or the way information is presented can affect suggestibility. For example, suggestive questions or leading information can distort our perceptions and memories. Similarly, repeated exposure to a suggestion or idea can increase its influence, a phenomenon known as the illusion of truth effect.

Finally, certain states or conditions can enhance suggestibility, such as fatigue, stress, hypnosis, or altered states of consciousness. For example, research has shown that suggestibility is generally higher during hypnosis or when individuals are sleep-deprived or under the influence of certain drugs.

Suggestibility is a complex and multifaceted phenomenon that can significantly influence our perceptions, memories, and beliefs, including those related to encounters with Sasquatch. Understanding and recognizing the factors that can increase suggestibility can help us to critically evaluate and verify our experiences and the information we receive from others.

External Influences and Leading Questions

External influences, such as media coverage, social pressure, or leading questions from investigators, can significantly impact eyewitness testimony. Media portrayals of Sasquatch and the desire for attention or validation can shape witnesses' recollections, leading to the unintentional fabrication or embellishment of details. Similarly, investigators' questioning techniques can inadvertently introduce biases or suggest certain responses, further compromising the reliability of eyewitness accounts.

External influences and leading questions are two significant factors that can shape and manipulate an individual's perception, memory, and recounting of an event. In the context of encounters with a Sasquatch, these factors can significantly influence the credibility and accuracy of eyewitness accounts.

External influences refer to factors outside of an individual that can affect their perception and interpretation of an event. These can include social, cultural, and environmental factors, as well as media exposure. For instance, an individual who has been exposed to stories, movies, or documentaries about Sasquatch might be more likely to interpret an ambiguous encounter in the wilderness as a Sasquatch sighting. Similarly, cultural beliefs or societal expectations can also shape an individual's interpretation of their experiences. For example, in areas where belief in Sasquatch is common, individuals might be more likely to report sightings.

Leading questions are questions that are phrased in a way that suggests a particular answer. They can subtly guide an individual's memory or perception of an event, often without the individual realizing it. For example, asking an eyewitness "Did you see the Sasquatch's large, hairy feet?" suggests that the creature they saw was a Sasquatch and that it had large, hairy feet. This can lead the eyewitness to recall seeing these specific details, even if they did not actually observe them.

In the context of Sasquatch encounters, external influences, and leading questions can significantly shape eyewitness accounts. For instance, an individual who has been exposed to a lot of Sasquatch-related media might interpret an encounter with an unidentified creature as a Sasquatch sighting. Similarly, if an interviewer asks leading questions during an eyewitness interview, it can shape the eyewitness's memory of the event and lead them to recall details that align with the interviewer's suggestions.

For example, if an eyewitness is asked, "Did the creature you saw have long, ape-like arms, like a Sasquatch?" instead of "Can you describe the creature's arms?" the eyewitness might recall the creature having long, ape-like arms, even if this is not what they originally observed. This can lead to inaccurate or embellished eyewitness accounts, which can further perpetuate myths and misconceptions about Sasquatch.

Similar to other factors we have covered, external influences and leading questions can significantly shape and manipulate an individual's perception, memory, and recounting of an event. In the context of Sasquatch encounters, these factors can lead to inaccurate or embellished eyewitness accounts, which can further perpetuate myths and misconceptions about this creature.

Eyewitness testimony, including Sasquatch sightings, must be approached with caution due to its inherent unreliability. Memory and recall, perception and interpretation, attention and focus, suggestibility, and confirmation bias, as well as external influences and leading questions, all contribute to the fallibility of eyewitnesses.

To mitigate the unreliability of eyewitness testimony, researchers and investigators must employ rigorous methods, including corroborating evidence, multiple witnesses, and independent verification. By recognizing the limitations of eyewitness accounts and adopting a critical and evidence-based approach, we can strive for a more accurate understanding of Sasquatch and other phenomena, ultimately advancing our knowledge in the field of cryptozoology.

There are several strategies that researchers can employ to mitigate these issues and increase the reliability of eyewitness accounts.

Detailed Interviews: Conducting thorough and detailed interviews is crucial. Researchers should ask open-ended questions that allow the witness to describe their experience in their own words. This can provide valuable context and details that may not emerge in a more structured interview.

Specific Questions: Researchers should ask specific questions about the encounter. For example, they could ask about the time of day, the weather conditions, the witness's location, and what they were doing at the time of the sighting. They should also ask about the creature's appearance, behavior, and any sounds it made.

Cross-Verification: If possible, researchers should seek to cross-verify the witness's account with other evidence. This could include physical evidence, such as footprints or hair samples, or other eyewitness accounts from the same area and time period.

Expert Consultation: Researchers should consult with experts in relevant fields, such as wildlife biology or acoustics, to help interpret the evidence. These experts can provide valuable insights and may be able to identify known animals or sounds that could have been mistaken for a Sasquatch.

Psychological Assessment: Researchers should consider the psychological state of the witness. Factors such as stress, fatigue, or the influence of alcohol or drugs can affect perception and memory. If the witness was in a heightened emotional state at the time of the sighting, this could increase the likelihood of pareidolia or misidentification.

Consideration of Pareidolia: Researchers should specifically ask about the conditions that could lead to auditory or visual pareidolia. For example, they could ask if the witness was actively looking for or expecting to see a Sasquatch, as this could increase the likelihood of pareidolia.

Training and Education: Researchers should educate themselves and their witnesses about the common sources of misidentification in the wilderness. This could include known animals, natural phenomena, and the effects of pareidolia.

By employing these strategies, Sasquatch researchers can increase the reliability of eyewitness accounts and improve their ability to distinguish between genuine Sasquatch encounters and cases of pareidolia or misidentification. However, it's important to remember that even with these strategies, eyewitness accounts are still subject to human error and bias and should always be considered as part of a larger body of evidence.

Pareidolia and misidentification will always pose significant challenges in the search for Sasquatch. The power of pattern recognition and the fallibility of eyewitness accounts can lead to false positives and misinterpretations. Understanding the complexities of perception, the influence of cultural expectations, and the potential for misidentification is crucial for researchers and enthusiasts alike.

To navigate these challenges, it is essential to approach Sasquatch evidence with critical thinking, skepticism, and rigorous investigation. By acknowledging the potential for pareidolia and misidentification, researchers can strive for a more objective and evidence-based approach to Sasquatch research, ultimately working towards a deeper understanding of the phenomenon.

8

———————

THE SCIENTIFIC METHOD

We often speak of the use of the scientific method in the course of Sasquatch research, but the cold hard truth is that very few field investigators actually know what it is. The scientific method is a systematic approach used by scientists to investigate and understand the natural world. It involves a series of steps that help researchers formulate hypotheses, conduct experiments, analyze data, and draw conclusions. The development of the scientific method can be traced back to ancient civilizations, but it was refined and formalized during the Scientific Revolution during the 16th and 17th centuries.

One of the key figures in the development of the scientific method was Sir Francis Bacon, an English philosopher and statesman. Bacon emphasized the importance of empirical evidence and advocated for a systematic approach to scientific inquiry. His work laid the foundation for the scientific method as we know it today.

Another influential figure in the development of the scientific method was Sir Isaac Newton, an English physicist and mathematician. Newton's laws of motion and universal gravitation demonstrated the power of using mathematical principles to explain natural phenomena. His work exemplified the importance of observation, experimentation, and mathematical analysis in scientific research.

Over time, other scientists and philosophers contributed to the refinement of the scientific method. Karl Popper, a 20th-century philosopher of science, introduced the concept of falsifiability, which states that scientific theories must be testable and potentially disprovable. This criterion helped establish a clear demarcation between scientific and non-scientific claims.

Now, let's explore how the scientific method can be applied to collecting DNA, hair, and other evidence in Sasquatch research. While the existence of Sasquatch of course remains unproven, some researchers have attempted to gather evidence using scientific methods.

To apply the scientific method in Sasquatch research, scientists would first formulate a hypothesis, such as "Sasquatch exists and leaves behind physical traces." They would then design repeatable experiments to collect evidence, such as setting up camera traps in areas with reported sightings or collecting hair samples found in potential Sasquatch habitats.

Once the evidence is collected, scientists would analyze it using various techniques. DNA analysis could be performed on hair samples to determine if they belong to an unknown primate species. This analysis would involve comparing the DNA sequences to known species and looking for any significant differences.

Researchers could examine the morphology and structure of the hair samples under a microscope to identify any unique characteristics. They might also analyze the isotopic composition of the hair to gain insights into the creature's diet and habitat.

Throughout this process, scientists should maintain rigorous documentation and transparency, ensuring that their methods and findings can be replicated and verified by other researchers. This is a crucial aspect of the scientific method, as it promotes objectivity and minimizes biases.

The scientific method is a powerful tool that has been developed and refined over centuries. It provides a systematic approach to investigating the natural world and has been instrumental in advancing our understanding of various phenomena. When applied to Sasquatch research, the scientific method can help researchers collect and analyze evidence, potentially shedding light on the existence of this elusive creature.

There are very few trained scientists who are willing to take a serious look at the possibility of a relic hominid roaming the vast wilderness of North America. The average Sasquatch researcher is just like you and me: weekend warriors, with a passion for the subject, getting out into the woods when they can.

What we need are more citizen scientists. A citizen scientist is an individual who actively participates in scientific research and data collection, typically without formal scientific training. They contribute their time, effort, and expertise to assist professional scientists in conducting research and gathering data. Citizen scientists play a crucial role in various fields, including ecology, astronomy, and even cryptozoology, such as Sasquatch research.

In the context of Sasquatch research, citizen scientists can contribute in several ways. Firstly, they can report sightings and encounters with potential Sasquatch creatures. These reports provide valuable anecdotal evidence that can help researchers identify areas of interest and focus their investigations. Citizen scientists can document their observations, noting the date, time, location, and any relevant details about the encounter, such as the creature's appearance, behavior, and any physical evidence left behind.

Citizen scientists can certainly assist in setting up and maintaining camera traps or other monitoring equipment in areas with reported Sasquatch activity. These devices can capture images or videos of potential Sasquatch sightings, providing visual evidence that can be analyzed by researchers. Citizen scientists can help deploy and retrieve these devices, ensuring they are properly positioned and functioning correctly.

In addition to visual evidence, citizen scientists can also collect physical evidence, such as hair samples, footprints, or scat, if they come across any during their explorations. They can carefully document the location, take photographs, and collect samples following proper protocols to preserve the integrity of the evidence. This evidence can then be analyzed by professional scientists using various techniques, including DNA analysis, to determine its origin and potentially identify any unknown species.

Citizen scientists can also contribute to Sasquatch research by participating in data analysis. They can help review and categorize camera trap images, identify potential Sasquatch features or behaviors, and contribute to the development of databases or online platforms where sightings and evidence can be recorded and shared. By collectively analyzing and interpreting data, citizen scientists can help identify patterns, trends, or correlations that may provide insights into the existence and behavior of Sasquatch.

It is important to note that while citizen scientists can make significant contributions to Sasquatch research, their involvement should be guided by scientific principles and methodologies. Collaboration with professional scientists and adherence to established protocols ensure that data collection and analysis are rigorous and reliable. This collaboration also allows for the integration of citizen science findings with existing scientific knowledge, enhancing the overall understanding of Sasquatch as a potential species.

One of the biggest hurdles in Sasquatch research as I see it, is confirmation bias. Confirmation bias is a cognitive bias that refers to the tendency of individuals to interpret and seek out information in a way that confirms their preexisting beliefs or hypotheses while disregarding or downplaying contradictory evidence. It is a natural human tendency to seek confirmation of what we already believe, as it provides a sense of validation and reinforces our existing worldview.

Confirmation bias is a psychological phenomenon where individuals tend to favor, seek, interpret, and remember information that confirms their pre-existing beliefs or values. It is a type of cognitive bias and a systematic error of inductive reasoning. This bias can lead to faulty decision-making as it can cause one to overlook or ignore information that contradicts their beliefs.

This bias can manifest in various ways. For instance, when researching a particular topic, individuals may only pay attention to sources that support their viewpoint while disregarding those that challenge it. Similarly, in a conversation or debate, people might only hear and remember arguments that align with their perspective, ignoring or dismissing counterarguments.

Confirmation bias can significantly affect individuals who are unaware they are practicing it. It can limit their perspective, making them less open to new ideas or alternative viewpoints. This can lead to a lack of understanding and empathy towards others with different beliefs or opinions.

In decision-making processes, confirmation bias can lead to poor or misguided decisions as it prevents individuals from fully considering all relevant information. It can also contribute to overconfidence in personal beliefs and can reinforce stereotypes and contribute to social prejudice.

In the context of problem-solving, confirmation bias can prevent individuals from finding the best solution as they may only consider evidence that supports their initial idea and ignore evidence suggesting other solutions.

In the realm of science and research, confirmation bias can lead to erroneous conclusions if researchers only pay attention to data that supports their hypothesis and overlook data that contradicts it.

Overall, confirmation bias can hinder critical thinking, objective analysis, and balanced judgment. It can lead to polarization in social and political contexts and can perpetuate misinformation and false beliefs. Therefore, it's crucial to be aware of and actively counteract confirmation bias to ensure more accurate understanding and decision-making.

In the context of Sasquatch field research, confirmation bias can have a significant negative impact. As researchers and enthusiasts who engage in Sasquatch field research, we often have a strong belief in the existence of this creature. Confirmation bias can influence our approach and interpretation of evidence.

One way confirmation bias affects Sasquatch field research is through the selection and interpretation of evidence. Researchers may actively seek out information, eyewitness accounts, or physical evidence that supports the existence of Sasquatch while ignoring or dismissing evidence that contradicts their beliefs. For example, they may focus on eyewitness testimonies that describe sightings of a large, hairy creature, while disregarding accounts that can be explained by other natural phenomena or misidentifications.

Confirmation bias can also impact the way researchers analyze and interpret ambiguous or inconclusive evidence. In the case of Sasquatch, evidence often includes blurry photographs, indistinct footprints, or audio recordings of unidentified sounds. Confirmation bias can lead researchers to interpret such evidence in a way that aligns with their preexisting beliefs. They may see patterns or details that confirm the existence of Sasquatch, even when alternative explanations or mundane origins are more plausible.

Confirmation bias can influence the design and execution of research methodologies. Researchers may unintentionally design studies or surveys that are more likely to yield positive results, inadvertently biasing the data in favor of their beliefs. They may also selectively report or emphasize findings that support their hypotheses while downplaying or omitting contradictory evidence. This can lead to a skewed perception of the overall body of evidence, as it becomes unrepresentative and biased towards confirming the existence of Sasquatch.

Sasquatch field research suffers greatly when researchers allow their bias to hinder scientific progress by impeding objective analysis and interpretation of evidence. Confirmation bias prevents researchers from critically evaluating all available information, which is essential for advancing knowledge and understanding. It can also lead to the perpetuation of pseudoscientific practices, as researchers may prioritize confirming their beliefs over rigorous scientific inquiry.

Confirmation bias can contribute to the perpetuation of myths and misinformation surrounding Sasquatch. When researchers selectively present evidence that supports the existence of Sasquatch, it can influence public perception and reinforce the belief in this creature. This can lead to a proliferation of unreliable information, sensationalism, and the spread of unfounded claims, ultimately hindering the credibility and reputation of Bigfoot field research as a whole. Overcoming confirmation bias is crucial for conducting objective and rigorous research, ensuring the integrity of scientific inquiry, and promoting a more accurate understanding of the natural world.

Good solid research requires conscious effort and a commitment to objectivity. Here are some strategies and good practices to help mitigate its impact.

Awareness: Recognize that confirmation bias exists and acknowledge that it can influence your thinking and research. Be aware of your own preexisting beliefs and how they may shape your interpretation of evidence.

Seek diverse perspectives: Actively seek out and consider alternative viewpoints, theories, and explanations. Engage with researchers and experts who hold different opinions or have different interpretations of the evidence. This helps to broaden your understanding and challenge your own biases.

Embrace skepticism: Cultivate a healthy skepticism towards your own beliefs and hypotheses. Question your assumptions and be open to the possibility of being wrong. Adopting a skeptical mindset encourages critical thinking and helps to counteract confirmation bias.

Use rigorous research methodologies: Design your research methodologies in a way that minimizes bias and maximizes objectivity. Ensure that your study design is robust, controls for confounding variables, and includes appropriate control groups or comparison groups. This helps to reduce the influence of bias on your findings.

Blind analysis: Consider implementing blind analysis techniques, where the researchers analyzing the data are unaware of the hypothesis or expected outcomes. This helps to prevent bias from influencing the interpretation of results.

Seek out contradictory evidence: Actively search for evidence that contradicts your beliefs or hypotheses. Give equal weight and consideration to both supporting and contradictory evidence. This helps to ensure a balanced and comprehensive evaluation of the available information.

Peer review and collaboration: Engage in peer review and collaborate with other researchers in your field. Seek feedback and input from colleagues who may have different perspectives or expertise. This helps to ensure that your research is subjected to critical evaluation and helps to minimize bias.

Transparency and replication: Be transparent in your research methods, data collection, and analysis. Clearly document your procedures and make your data available for scrutiny and replication by other researchers. This promotes transparency, and accountability, and also helps to mitigate bias.

Continuous learning: Stay updated with the latest research, methodologies, and advancements in your field. Attend conferences, read scientific journals, and engage in discussions with experts. Continuous learning helps to refine your research skills, broaden your knowledge, and reduce the impact of bias.

One of the keys to avoiding confirmation bias in your research is the practice of critical thinking. Critical thinking by definition, is a cognitive process that involves the analysis, evaluation, and synthesis of information gathered through observation, experience, reflection, or communication. It is a disciplined intellectual process that actively and skillfully conceptualizes, applies, analyzes, synthesizes, and evaluates information gathered from, or generated by, observation, experience, reflection, reasoning, or communication, as a guide to belief and action. It involves the ability to reason logically and to identify, evaluate, and construct arguments, and it requires skepticism, open-mindedness, and the ability to think clearly and rationally.

The origins of critical thinking can be traced back to the teachings of Socrates, recorded by Plato around 2,500 years ago. Socrates established the importance of seeking evidence, closely examining reasoning and assumptions, analyzing basic concepts, and tracing out implications. The tradition of critical thinking was carried forward by philosophers such as Aristotle and the Stoics, and it was later incorporated into the scientific method developed during the scientific revolution.

Critical thinking is closely related to the scientific method, a systematic approach to acquiring knowledge that involves careful observation, formulation of hypotheses, conducting experiments to test these hypotheses, and drawing conclusions based on the results. Both critical thinking and the scientific method require objectivity, logical reasoning, and the ability to question assumptions and evaluate evidence.

Applying critical thinking to Sasquatch research involves several steps. First, one must gather all available evidence, which may include eyewitness accounts, physical evidence such as footprints or hair samples, and any available photographic or video evidence. This evidence must then be analyzed critically, questioning the reliability of the sources and the validity of the evidence itself.

For example, eyewitness accounts can be subject to memory errors or misinterpretations, and physical evidence can be contaminated or misidentified. Photographic and video evidence must be scrutinized for possible tampering or misinterpretation. Any hypotheses about the existence or nature of Sasquatch must be based on this critical evaluation of the evidence.

Next, these hypotheses must be tested. This could involve further field research to gather more evidence, or experiments to test specific aspects of the hypotheses. For example, if a hypothesis proposes that Sasquatch is a nocturnal creature, night-time surveillance in areas with frequent sightings could be conducted.

Finally, the results of these tests must be analyzed and conclusions drawn. If the evidence supports the hypotheses, they may be accepted as tentative explanations, but they must remain open to further testing and revision in light of new evidence. If the evidence does not support the hypotheses, they must be rejected or revised.

Despite its importance, critical thinking is not as common as one might expect. A study by the American Institutes for Research found that only 28% of college graduates were rated proficient in critical thinking. This lack of critical thinking can be seen in various fields, including the research and study of Sasquatch, also known as Bigfoot.

In Sasquatch research, critical thinking plays a pivotal role in separating fact from fiction, evidence from anecdotes, and science from pseudoscience. It allows researchers to objectively evaluate claims, scrutinize evidence, and question assumptions. Without critical thinking, researchers may fall prey to cognitive biases, logical fallacies, and misinformation, leading to flawed conclusions and misguided beliefs.

The lack of critical thinking in Sasquatch research can significantly affect how the phenomenon is viewed by both believers and skeptics. For believers, the absence of critical thinking can lead to uncritical acceptance of dubious claims, uncritical interpretation of ambiguous evidence, and uncritical adherence to unfounded beliefs. This can result in a distorted view of the phenomenon, a misguided understanding of the evidence, and a misplaced faith in pseudoscientific theories.

For skeptics, the lack of critical thinking can lead to uncritical dismissal of credible claims, uncritical rejection of compelling evidence, and uncritical adherence to debunked theories. This can result in a dismissive attitude towards the phenomenon, a biased interpretation of the evidence, and a dogmatic belief in scientific orthodoxy.

The failure to apply critical thinking can also affect the public perception of Sasquatch research. For the general public, the uncritical acceptance of dubious claims by believers can reinforce the stereotype of Sasquatch researchers as gullible and credulous. Conversely, the uncritical dismissal of credible claims by skeptics can reinforce the stereotype of Sasquatch researchers as closed-minded and dogmatic.

Scientific literacy involves understanding the nature of science, the process of scientific inquiry, and the role of evidence in science. Intellectual humility involves recognizing the limits of one's knowledge, the fallibility of one's beliefs, and the uncertainty of one's conclusions. Skeptical inquiry involves questioning claims, scrutinizing evidence, and challenging assumptions.

Critical thinking is a vital life skill and should be employed in Sasquatch research. It allows researchers to objectively evaluate claims, scrutinize evidence, and question assumptions. The lack of critical thinking can lead to flawed conclusions, misguided beliefs, and distorted perceptions. To enhance critical thinking, it is essential to promote scientific literacy, foster intellectual humility, and cultivate skeptical inquiry.

Critical thinking is a valuable tool for any researcher, including those investigating the Sasquatch phenomenon. It involves the ability to analyze information objectively and make a reasoned judgment. It includes the ability to engage in reflective and independent thinking, understand the logical connections between ideas, detect inconsistencies and common mistakes in reasoning, solve problems systematically, identify the relevance and importance of ideas, and reflect on the justification of one's own beliefs and values.

Critical thinking can help Sasquatch researchers overcome confirmation bias in several ways.

Evaluation of Evidence: Critical thinking encourages researchers to evaluate all evidence with an open mind, rather than just focusing on evidence that supports their existing beliefs. This means considering the quality and reliability of the evidence, and whether it really supports the conclusions being drawn.

Questioning Assumptions: Critical thinking involves questioning assumptions. For Sasquatch researchers, this might mean questioning the assumption that Sasquatch exists, or that certain evidence (like footprints or hair samples) must come from a Sasquatch.

Considering Alternative Explanations: Critical thinking also involves considering alternative explanations. For example, if a researcher finds a large footprint in the woods, they might consider other explanations, such as it being made by a bear or a human prankster, rather than immediately assuming it was made by a Sasquatch.

Logical Reasoning: Critical thinking involves logical reasoning, which can help researchers avoid fallacies that can result from confirmation bias. For example, the fallacy of affirming the consequent involves reasoning that if a certain hypothesis is true, we would expect to see a certain piece of evidence, and since we see that piece of evidence, the hypothesis must be true. But this reasoning is fallacious because there could be other explanations for the evidence.

Reflective Thinking: Critical thinking involves reflective thinking, which can help researchers recognize their own biases and take steps to mitigate them. This might involve seeking out disconfirming evidence or consulting with others to get different perspectives.

Critical thinking in my opinion is key for Sasquatch researchers to overcome confirmation bias helps us evaluate all evidence objectively, question assumptions, consider alternative explanations, use logical reasoning, and engage in reflective thinking. This can help avoid common mistakes in reasoning and make more accurate and reliable conclusions about the Sasquatch phenomenon.

By consciously applying any or all these strategies, researchers can conduct good solid research that is objective, rigorous, and contributes to the advancement of knowledge in the field of Sasquatch research.

$$9$$

WHERE ARE THE BODIES?

The age-old argument for skepticism as it relates to the Sasquatch existence is where is the body. Cynics and skeptics argue that if Sasquatch truly exists, there should be concrete evidence in the form of a deceased body or skeletal remains. They question how a creature of such purported size and presence could have eluded human detection for centuries without leaving behind any tangible proof.

Proponents of the Sasquatch theory, on the other hand, offer several counterarguments to address this skepticism. They argue that the vast and remote wilderness areas where Sasquatch sightings occur make it highly unlikely for a body to be discovered. These regions are often inaccessible, densely forested, and home to numerous scavengers that would quickly disperse any remains.

Sasquatch enthusiasts often claim that the creature possesses a level of intelligence and elusiveness that allows it to avoid human contact and detection. They argue that Sasquatch may have developed sophisticated survival strategies, such as burying their dead or disposing of them in ways that prevent their discovery.

Another point raised by believers is the possibility that Sasquatch has a significantly lower population density, making encounters and subsequent deaths rare. They suggest that the creature's elusive nature and ability to navigate vast territories may contribute to its ability to avoid detection and minimize the chances of finding a body.

Skeptics often underestimate the challenges of conducting thorough scientific investigations in remote areas. The vastness of wilderness, limited resources, and the sheer difficulty of locating and studying an elusive creature like Sasquatch make it a daunting task. Lack of funding and scientific interest also contribute to the scarcity of comprehensive research on the subject.

Until more comprehensive scientific investigations are conducted, the debate surrounding the existence of Sasquatch will likely continue, with skeptics demanding a body and believers presenting alternative explanations for its absence.

Whether you are a skeptic or a hard-core believer the question about why remains have not been located is worth exploring further. From the perspective that Sasquatch is a living, breathing, flesh, and blood creature, several factors can help explain why Sasquatch remains have never been found. To understand this, we must again turn to history and take a look at the known fossil record of extant and extinct apes, as well as the intricate process of fossilization and the challenges it presents for finding fossils of large primates.

Extant and Extinct Ape Fossil Record

The fossil record of apes, both extant (currently living) and extinct, provides valuable insights into the challenges of finding remains. While numerous fossils of extinct apes have been discovered, the remains of extant apes are exceedingly rare. This scarcity is due to various factors, including the specific conditions required for fossilization, the habitats in which apes live, and the relatively recent divergence of ape lineages.

The study of ape species fossils provides valuable insights into the evolutionary history of primates, including humans. Here is an overview of the extant and extinct ape species fossils discovered to date, along with their distribution and representation in the known fossil record. It is important to note that new discoveries are constantly being made, and the information presented here represents the current understanding based on available data.

Extant Ape Species Fossils

Extant ape species refer to those that are still living today. There are currently seven recognized extant ape species, including humans (*Homo sapiens*), chimpanzees (*Pan troglodytes* and *Pan paniscus*), bonobos (*Pan paniscus*), gorillas (*Gorilla gorilla* and *Gorilla beringei*), orangutans (*Pongo pygmaeus* and *Pongo abelii*), and gibbons (family *Hylobatidae*).

Extinct Ape Species Fossils

a. *Proconsul*:

Proconsul is an extinct genus of ape that lived during the Miocene epoch, approximately 23 to 25 million years ago. Fossils of *Proconsul* have been found in East Africa, specifically in Kenya and Uganda. Several species have been identified, including *Proconsul africanus*, *Proconsul nyanzae*, and *Proconsul heseloni*.

b. *Dryopithecus*:

Dryopithecus is an extinct genus of ape that lived during the Miocene epoch, approximately 9 to 12 million years ago. Fossils of *Dryopithecus* have been discovered in Europe, primarily in France, Spain, and Germany.

c. *Gigantopithecus*:

Gigantopithecus is an extinct genus of ape that lived during the Pleistocene epoch, approximately nine million to one hundred thousand years ago. Fossils of *Gigantopithecus* have been found in Asia, particularly in China, India, and Vietnam. The species *Gigantopithecus blacki* is the most well-known and largest known ape species, estimated to have stood up to ten feet tall.

Representation of Ape Species in the Fossil Record

The known fossil record provides a glimpse into the diversity of life forms that have existed on Earth. However, it is important to note that the fossil record is incomplete, and many species may not be represented due to various factors such as fossilization biases, preservation conditions, and limited sampling.

The fossil record represents only a fraction of the total number of species that have ever lived. It is estimated that less than 1% of all species that have ever existed are represented in the known fossil record. This is known as the "Signor-Lipps effect," which suggests that the absence of a particular species in the fossil record does not necessarily indicate its non-existence.

The study of extant and extinct ape species fossils has provided valuable insights into the evolutionary history of primates. While the fossil record has revealed important information about the diversity and distribution of ape species, it is crucial to acknowledge its limitations. Ongoing research and new discoveries continue to expand our understanding of ape evolution, and future findings may shed further light on the fascinating history of these remarkable creatures.

Fossilization Process

Fossilization is a complex and rare process that occurs under specific conditions. For an organism to become fossilized, several factors must align:

a. Rapid Burial: Rapid burial is crucial in the fossilization process for several reasons. Firstly, it protects the remains of the organism from scavengers and decomposers that can quickly disintegrate and consume the body. This is particularly important for large organisms, such as dinosaurs or mammoths, whose remains are a rich source of nutrients for scavengers.

Secondly, rapid burial shields the remains from weathering and erosion, which can wear away and destroy the bones and other hard parts. By burying the remains, they are protected from the elements, increasing the chances of preservation.

Lastly, rapid burial creates an anoxic, or oxygen-poor, environment. This slows down the decomposition process and inhibits the activity of bacteria and other microorganisms that can break down the remains.

Rapid burial typically occurs in environments with high sediment deposition rates. These include riverbanks, lake beds, and ocean floors, where sediment carried by water can quickly cover the remains. Volcanic ash falls can also lead to rapid burial, as the ash can swiftly blanket and preserve the remains.

The type of sediment also plays a role in the burial process. Fine-grained sediments, such as clay and silt, are more effective at preserving details of the remains than coarse-grained sediments like sand or gravel.

The speed and manner of burial can significantly affect the quality of the resulting fossil. Rapid and gentle burial can preserve delicate structures and even soft tissues, leading to exceptionally detailed fossils. For instance, the fossils found in the Burgess Shale in Canada and the Chengjiang Maotianshan Shales in China, which were rapidly buried in fine-grained sediment, have preserved soft tissues and fine anatomical details.

In contrast, violent or slow burial can damage the remains or allow more time for decomposition and scavenging, resulting in less complete and detailed fossils.

While rapid burial is crucial for fossilization, it is also a rare event. Most organisms decompose or are scavenged before they can be buried. Moreover, the chances of rapid burial are lower in certain environments, such as forests, where sediment deposition rates are typically low.

Rapid burial plays a pivotal role in the fossilization process. It protects the remains from destruction, creates a conducive environment for preservation, and can enhance the quality of the resulting fossil. However, the rarity of rapid burial events and the specific conditions required make the fossilization process a rare and exceptional occurrence.

Sasquatch is often associated with dense, forested environments. These environments have low sediment deposition rates, making rapid burial unlikely. Leaves and other organic matter on the forest floor decompose quickly, returning nutrients to the soil rather than contributing to layers of sediment that could bury and preserve remains.

Sasquatch sightings are also commonly reported in mountainous areas. While landslides and avalanches can potentially lead to rapid burial, these events are sporadic and unpredictable. Moreover, the violent nature of these events can damage or disintegrate remains, reducing the chances of fossilization.

Forests and mountains are home to a variety of scavengers, from small insects to larger mammals. If a Sasquatch were to die in these environments, its remains would likely be quickly scattered or consumed by scavengers. Additionally, the moist and oxygen-rich conditions in these environments would accelerate the decomposition process.

Rapid burial creates anoxic, or oxygen-poor, conditions that slow down decomposition and inhibit the activity of bacteria and other microorganisms. However, the environments associated with Sasquatch are typically oxygen-rich, which would promote rather than inhibit decomposition.

If Sasquatch were to exist, it is often portrayed as a solitary creature with a low population density. This means there would be fewer individuals available to become fossils in the first place.

b. Favorable Environment: The burial site must possess conditions that promote fossilization, such as low oxygen levels, limited microbial activity, and the presence of minerals that aid in preserving the remains. As previously mentioned, these conditions are not commonly found in the environments where Sasquatch is believed to reside.

c. Geological Processes: Geological processes, such as sedimentation, compaction, and mineralization, transform the buried remains into fossils. Over time, more layers of sediment build up and the weight compresses the lower layers into rock. As the original organism decays, water seeping through the sediment carries minerals into or out of the remains. This can result in the replacement of the original organic material with minerals, a process known as permineralization. In some cases, the original material is completely replaced, creating a stone copy of the original organism, known as a cast or mold fossil.

However, not all organisms are equally likely to become fossilized. The process favors organisms with hard parts, such as bones, shells, or teeth. Soft-bodied organisms, like worms or jellyfish, are much less likely to leave behind fossils. The environment in which an organism dies can greatly affect its chances of fossilization. Organisms that die in areas with rapid sediment deposition, such as river deltas or the bottom of the sea, are more likely to be fossilized than those that die in other environments.

The remote, forested areas in North America, particularly the Pacific Northwest, are not conducive to fossilization for several reasons. First, forests are not typically areas of rapid sediment deposition. Instead, organic material tends to decompose quickly and be recycled back into the ecosystem. Second, the acidic soils common in many forest environments can accelerate the decomposition of bones and other hard parts. Finally, the remote and rugged nature of these areas makes the discovery of any potential fossils highly unlikely.

If Sasquatch is a primate as some suggest, it would be even less likely to leave behind fossils. Primates have a poor fossil record overall, due to their preference for forested habitats and their relatively low population densities. In fact, many known primate species are known only from a handful of fossil specimens. However, these processes are highly dependent on specific geological conditions, which may not align with the habitats frequented by Sasquatch.

Challenges in Finding Fossils of Large Primates

Even when the conditions for fossilization are met, finding fossils of large primates, including Sasquatch, presents additional challenges:

a. Scavengers and Decomposition: Scavengers and decomposition play a significant role in the fossilization process. When an organism dies, its remains are often quickly consumed by scavengers or decomposed by bacteria and other microorganisms. This rapid breakdown of organic material can prevent the formation of fossils, as fossilization requires the preservation of an organism's remains.

Large primates, such as gorillas and orangutans, are particularly susceptible to this process. Their large size makes them an attractive food source for a variety of scavengers, from large carnivores to small insects. Additionally, the humid, tropical environments where many large primates live are ideal for rapid decomposition. The combination of these factors can result in the complete destruction of a primate's remains in a matter of weeks or even days.

If Sasquatch is a large primate, it would likely face similar challenges to fossilization. Assuming Sasquatch lives in a similar environment to other large primates, its remains would be subject to rapid scavenging and decomposition. This could explain the lack of Sasquatch fossils despite numerous reported sightings of the creature.

It's important to note that the lack of Sasquatch fossils does not necessarily mean the creature does not exist. As I pointed out earlier fossil record is inherently incomplete, and many species are known only from a handful of fossils. It's also possible that Sasquatch fossils exist but have not yet been discovered or correctly identified.

b. Limited Fossilization Potential: The limited fossilization potential of large primates, including hominids, is due to several factors that make the preservation of their remains less likely than those of other species. This has significant implications for our understanding of primate evolution and the number of known primate fossils.

The habitats in which large primates typically live are not conducive to fossilization. Primates, including humans and their ancestors, tend to inhabit forested or jungle environments. When an organism dies in such an environment, its remains are likely to be quickly decomposed by the abundant life forms present, leaving little to no trace for potential fossilization. In contrast, organisms that live in environments such as river deltas or shallow seas are more likely to be quickly buried in sediment after death, which can protect their remains from decomposition and increase the chances of fossilization.

Another factor is the bones of large primates are relatively fragile and prone to decay. This is particularly true for the thin-walled bones of the skull, which are often of great interest to paleontologists. Even if a primate's remains are buried quickly after death, the bones may not survive the pressure of being buried under sediment for thousands or millions of years.

The population density of large primates is typically low, meaning that there are fewer individuals that could potentially become fossilized. This is in contrast to species with high population densities, such as many types of fish or small mammals, which are more likely to leave a substantial fossil record.

These factors combine to make the fossil record of large primates patchy and incomplete. This has implications for our understanding of primate evolution, as it means that there are likely many species and evolutionary transitions that we know nothing about due to the lack of fossil evidence.

As for the lack of Sasquatch fossils in the known fossil record, the limited fossilization potential of large primates could certainly be a contributing factor. If Sasquatches do or did exist, they will likely inhabit forested environments and have low population densities, both of which would reduce their chances of becoming fossilized. Some would argue that since there is currently no definitive scientific evidence to support the existence of Sasquatches, the lack of Sasquatch fossils could simply be because such creatures never existed.

c. Remote and Inaccessible Habitats: Remote and inaccessible habitats significantly affect the fossilization process and the subsequent discovery of large primate fossils. As we know, the process of fossilization is complex and requires a specific set of conditions to occur. These conditions are often not met in the habitats where large primates typically live, which are often remote, inaccessible, and not conducive to fossilization.

Large primates, including hominids, are known to inhabit forested or jungle environments. These environments are teeming with life forms that quickly decompose organic matter, including the remains of deceased animals. This rapid decomposition leaves little to no trace of the organism for potential fossilization.

The remote and inaccessible nature of these habitats also poses challenges for the discovery and extraction of fossils. Dense vegetation, difficult terrain, and the presence of dangerous wildlife can all hinder paleontological research in these areas. Even if a large primate dies in a location where its remains could potentially be fossilized, the chances of paleontologists finding and successfully extracting these fossils are slim due to these logistical challenges.

While the absence of Sasquatch remains or bones may raise doubts about their existence, considering the challenges associated with finding fossils of large primates provides a plausible explanation. The rarity of extant ape fossils, the intricate process of fossilization, and the specific challenge in finding remains of large primates all contribute to the mystery surrounding Sasquatch. Until further evidence emerges, the existence of Sasquatch will continue to be a subject of speculation and fascination.

THE ELUSIVENESS OF SASQUATCH: PRIMATE BEHAVIORS THAT AID IN STEALTH

The concept of an eight-foot-tall, hairy, bipedal primate going unnoticed in North America is a perplexing notion for most. Could it be as simple as their primate behaviors that allow them to hide in plain sight?

To unravel the mystery of Sasquatch's elusiveness, we must first examine what we do know about the evolutionary adaptations that primates possess. Primates, including humans, have evolved over millions of years to survive in diverse environments. Their physical characteristics, such as fur, coloration, and body structure, often aid in camouflage and blending with their surroundings. Sasquatch, if it exists, may have developed similar adaptations to remain concealed within its habitat.

Many primates, such as certain species of monkeys and apes, exhibit nocturnal behavior. This adaptation allows them to avoid direct competition with diurnal species and reduces their exposure to potential predators. Sasquatch sightings are often reported during the twilight hours or at night, suggesting that it may possess similar nocturnal tendencies. By remaining active during low-light conditions, Sasquatch could exploit the cover of darkness to move stealthily and avoid human encounters.

Numerous primates are adept climbers, spending a significant portion of their lives in trees. This arboreal lifestyle provides them with an advantage in terms of both safety and foraging opportunities. Sasquatch, if they exist, may possess similar climbing abilities, allowing them to navigate dense forests and evade detection by moving through the treetops. This behavior would enable Sasquatch to remain hidden from ground-level observers, making it even more challenging to spot.

Primates are known for their complex social structures, which often involve hierarchical relationships and intricate communication systems. These dynamics play a crucial role in their survival, as they facilitate cooperation, protection, and sharing of resources. If Sasquatch is a social creature, it may employ similar strategies to avoid human detection. By maintaining a network of individuals, Sasquatch could share information about potential threats, allowing them to adapt their behavior and remain hidden.

Many primates exhibit territorial behavior, marking and defending their home ranges against intruders. Sasquatch, if it exists, may employ similar territoriality to avoid human contact. By establishing and defending specific areas, Sasquatch can minimize the chances of encountering humans, who often venture into its habitat. Additionally, Sasquatch may possess an innate ability to sense human presence, allowing it to avoid areas frequented by humans altogether.

Primates communicate through a variety of vocalizations, including calls, hoots, and screams. Some species even possess the ability to mimic other animals or environmental sounds. Sasquatch, if real, may utilize similar vocalizations to communicate with its kind or deceive humans. By mimicking natural sounds or other animals, Sasquatch could further confuse and deter potential observers, making it harder to pinpoint its exact location.

I would be remiss if I failed to mention the lowland gorilla. Despite their immense size and strength, these remarkable primates managed to evade detection for centuries, leaving scientists and explorers puzzled. A native to the dense rainforests of Central and West Africa, the lowland gorilla remained hidden from human eyes until the late 19th century. Their remarkable ability to blend seamlessly into their environment, coupled with their cautious behavior and remote habitat, contributed to their prolonged concealment. Similarly, Sasquatch, often associated with North American forests, is believed to employ similar strategies to avoid human detection. By examining the history of the lowland gorilla, we can draw parallels and speculate on the methods Sasquatch may employ to remain elusive.

The lowland gorilla's natural habitat, dense rainforests, certainly played a crucial role in their ability to avoid detection. These vast and impenetrable forests provided the perfect cover for these elusive creatures. Explorers and scientists faced immense challenges in navigating through the dense vegetation, making it difficult to stumble upon gorilla populations. Similarly, Sasquatch is believed to inhabit remote and inaccessible regions, such as deep forests or mountainous areas, where human presence is limited.

Lowland gorillas possess a remarkable ability to blend into their surroundings. Their dark fur, which absorbs light, allows them to seamlessly merge with the shadows of the forest. Additionally, their stooped posture and stillness make them appear like part of the foliage. This camouflage technique, combined with their ability to mimic the sounds of the forest, enables them to remain undetected. Sasquatch sightings often describe a creature with similar camouflage abilities, blending into the forest environment and mimicking natural sounds to avoid detection.

Lowland gorillas are primarily diurnal, meaning they are active during the day. However, they exhibit a crepuscular behavior pattern, being most active during dawn and dusk. This behavior allows them to take advantage of the low light conditions, further enhancing their ability to remain hidden. Similarly, Sasquatch sightings often occur during twilight hours, suggesting a preference for low-light conditions to avoid human detection.

The lowland gorilla's ability to avoid detection for centuries can be attributed to a combination of factors, including their remote habitat, camouflage and mimicry techniques, and crepuscular behavior. These strategies have allowed them to remain hidden from human eyes until the late 19th century. Drawing parallels to Sasquatch, we can speculate that similar methods may be employed by this elusive creature to evade human detection. While the existence of Sasquatch remains a subject of debate, studying the history of the lowland gorilla provides valuable insights into the potential strategies employed by cryptids like Sasquatch to remain hidden from human observation.

11

HUMAN POPULATION GROWTH AND WILDERNESS LAND LOSS

Sasquatch going undiscovered in North America is one thing, but having a place to thrive is something else entirely. As the human population continues to grow at an unprecedented rate, encroaching upon previously untouched wilderness areas, the elusive Sasquatch faces increasing challenges in remaining an undiscovered species. By examining the effects of habitat loss, increased human presence, technological advancements, and the spread of urbanization, we can gain insights into the potential consequences of the continued elusiveness of Sasquatch.

Over the past two decades, the human population in the continental United States has experienced steady growth. According to the United States Census Bureau, the population in 2000 was approximately 282 million, which increased to around 331 million by 2020. This represents an overall population growth of approximately 17.4% during this period.

The rapid population growth in the continental United States has resulted in the loss of significant wilderness land. However, it is important to differentiate between designated wilderness areas and undeveloped or natural lands. Designated wilderness areas are protected by law and managed to preserve their natural state, while undeveloped or natural lands may not have the same level of legal protection.

The exact extent of wilderness land loss due to population growth is challenging to quantify precisely. However, urbanization, infrastructure development, agriculture expansion, and resource extraction have collectively contributed to the conversion of wilderness areas into developed or modified landscapes. This includes the construction of residential areas, roads, commercial zones, and industrial facilities.

Despite the loss of wilderness land, there are still significant areas in the continental United States that remain relatively untouched by human activities. These areas include national parks, national forests, wildlife refuges, and other protected lands. The United States has a diverse range of ecosystems and landscapes, providing potential sanctuaries for various species, including the hypothetical Sasquatch.

The exact extent of untouched wilderness land varies across different regions. For instance, Alaska, with its vast expanses of wilderness, offers substantial areas that remain largely untouched by human activities. Additionally, states such as Montana, Wyoming, Idaho, and parts of the Pacific Northwest still possess significant stretches of pristine wilderness.

The concept of Sasquatch remains speculative to most and lacks scientific evidence. However, if such a species were to exist, the remaining untouched wilderness areas could potentially offer sanctuary. These areas provide undisturbed habitats, abundant resources, and limited human presence, which could support the survival and protection of any elusive species.

Conservation efforts, including the establishment and expansion of protected areas, can contribute to preserving wilderness land and potentially provide refuge for any undiscovered or endangered species. These efforts involve habitat restoration, wildlife corridors, and sustainable land management practices to maintain the ecological integrity of these areas.

The facts do not lie. Despite the human population in the continental United States experiencing significant growth over the last two decades, resulting in the loss of wilderness land due to urbanization and development, there are substantial areas of untouched wilderness that still exist, offering potential sanctuaries for various species. While the existence of the Sasquatch remains speculative, the preservation and expansion of protected areas can contribute to the conservation of wilderness land and potentially provide refuge for any undiscovered or endangered species. Continued research, conservation efforts, and responsible land management are crucial to maintaining the ecological balance and protecting the remaining wilderness areas.

Even though these wilderness areas exist, human population growth often results in the destruction and fragmentation of natural habitats, reducing the available space for wildlife, including Sasquatch. As their habitats shrink, Sasquatch populations may become isolated, making it harder for them to maintain genetic diversity and increasing the risk of local extinctions. The loss and fragmentation of suitable habitats also limit the areas where Sasquatch can hide and thrive, making them more vulnerable to human detection.

With a growing human population, more people are venturing into previously remote and unexplored areas. This increased human presence poses a significant challenge to the elusiveness of Sasquatch. As humans encroach upon Sasquatch habitats, the likelihood of encounters and sightings rises. However, the fear and skepticism surrounding Sasquatch, coupled with the rarity of sightings, often lead to dismissals or misidentifications. Nevertheless, the increased human presence raises the risk of accidental discoveries or encounters that could potentially expose Sasquatch to further scrutiny.

Advancements in technology -- such as satellite imagery, drones, and trail cameras -- have revolutionized wildlife monitoring and surveying techniques. These tools provide researchers with unprecedented access to remote areas and enable them to gather data more efficiently. As technology continues to improve, the chances of capturing evidence of Sasquatch, in the form of clear photographs or videos, increase. Additionally, the use of thermal imaging and DNA analysis techniques may aid in detecting and confirming the presence of Sasquatch. The growth of the human population indirectly fuels technological advancements, potentially narrowing the gap between Sasquatch's elusiveness and scientific discovery.

As human populations expand, urbanization spreads, leading to the development of cities, towns, and infrastructure. Urban areas create noise, light pollution, and increased human activity, which can disrupt wildlife and drive them away from their natural habitats. Sasquatch, if it exists, may be particularly sensitive to human disturbance, further pushing them into remote and inaccessible regions. The spread of urbanization limits the available areas for Sasquatch to remain hidden, increasing the chances of human encounters and reducing their chances of remaining undiscovered.

Human population growth also influences cultural shifts and belief systems. As societies become more urbanized and modernized, traditional beliefs and folklore surrounding Sasquatch may diminish. This shift in cultural attitudes may lead to a decline in interest and support for Sasquatch research and conservation efforts. With fewer resources dedicated to studying and protecting Sasquatch, the chances of discovering and understanding this elusive species diminish.

The growth of the human population undoubtedly poses significant challenges to the continued elusiveness of Sasquatch. Habitat loss, increased human presence, technological advancements, urbanization, and cultural shifts all contribute to the potential exposure and decline of this mysterious species. As humans continue to encroach upon wilderness areas and exploit natural resources, the chances of discovering Sasquatch increase. However, the complex nature of their behavior, coupled with the vast and remote landscapes they inhabit, may still provide them with a slim chance of remaining hidden. Only through responsible conservation efforts, scientific research, and a balance between human development and wildlife preservation can we hope to protect the Sasquatch and ensure its continued existence as an undiscovered or discovered species.

12

─────────

CAN WE CONVICT SASQUATCH IN A COURT OF LAW?

In my previous career as a law enforcement officer, I spent a significant portion of my sixteen years dealing with facts and evidence. The role of a police officer often involves assisting in the prosecution of those they apprehend. This investigative process assures that convictions are not based on mere rumors or conjecture. The outcome of any court case hinges on the strength of facts and evidence. I've often jokingly remarked that if the existence of Sasquatch were on trial, it would undoubtedly be found guilty and in jail by now.

I've had numerous discussions with fellow researchers and Sasquatch enthusiasts who assert that there is ample evidence to confirm the existence of Sasquatch. However, for every believer, there are three doubters who argue that there is no proof of Sasquatch's existence. Interestingly, I've noticed that many researchers and skeptics alike seem to lack a fundamental understanding of what constitutes evidence and how many different forms it can take. With this in mind, I've decided to take a look at the various types of evidence that can be gathered and how certain examples may indicate the existence of a bipedal relic hominid in North America and other parts of the globe.

Real Evidence: Its Role in Proving the Existence of Sasquatch

Real evidence, also known as physical evidence, is any tangible object that can be perceived by the senses and presented in a court of law. It is a crucial component of legal proceedings, providing a concrete, often indisputable basis for arguments.

Real evidence can take many forms, including but not limited to fingerprints, DNA samples, tire impressions, and fingerprints. It is unique in that it is a direct piece of evidence, meaning it does not rely on human testimony or interpretation to establish its relevance. Instead, it is the evidence itself that speaks to the facts at issue.

In a court of law, real evidence is used to corroborate or refute the testimonies of witnesses, to establish a fact, or to provide a visual or tactile aid to the jury. For instance, a murder weapon with the defendant's fingerprints can directly link them to the crime scene, providing a strong argument for their guilt.

However, the use of real evidence is not without its challenges. It must be relevant to the case, meaning it must have a logical connection to the facts being disputed. It must also be authentic, meaning it must be proven to be what it purports to be. This is often established through a chain of custody, which documents the evidence's collection, handling, and preservation from the crime scene to the courtroom.

Real evidence must pass the rules of admissibility, which vary from jurisdiction to jurisdiction. Generally, it must be reliable, and its probative value must outweigh any potential prejudicial effect. For instance, gruesome photographs from a crime scene may be excluded if they are deemed to unduly influence the jury's emotions.

Now, let's turn to the intriguing world of cryptids, creatures whose existence is often disputed due to lack of substantial evidence. Sasquatch, or Bigfoot, is a prime example. Despite numerous sightings and anecdotal accounts, the scientific community largely dismisses its existence due to the absence of real evidence.

To prove the existence of Sasquatch using real evidence, one would need to present tangible, verifiable proof. This could take the form of physical remains, such as bones or hair, which could be subjected to DNA analysis. Clear, high-quality photographs or videos could also serve as real evidence, provided they can withstand scrutiny for authenticity.

However, the challenges are significant. Any physical remains would need to be indisputably linked to an unknown creature, ruling out the misidentification of known animals. Photographs or videos would need to be clear and detailed enough to rule out hoaxes or misinterpretations.

Additionally, the evidence would need to be compelling enough to overcome the inherent skepticism towards cryptids. This is where the *probative value* (the probability of evidence reaching its proof purpose of a relevant fact in issue) versus the *prejudicial effect* (the extent to which the evidence arouses the emotions of the jury such as sympathy or bias) comes into play. The evidence must be so compelling that its value in proving the existence of Sasquatch outweighs the potential prejudice of dismissing it as a mere myth.

Real evidence plays a pivotal role in the courtroom, providing a tangible basis for arguments. Its potential application in proving the existence of cryptids is intriguing, albeit fraught with challenges. Despite the challenges, the quest for real evidence of Sasquatch continues, fueled by the tantalizing possibility of uncovering one of nature's greatest mysteries.

Documentary Evidence: Its Role in Sasquatch Research

Documentation evidence, also known as documentary evidence, is a critical component in the legal system and scientific research. It refers to any evidence introduced at a trial in the form of documents. These documents can be anything from written letters, contracts, and invoices to digital files, such as emails, text messages, or social media posts. In essence, documentary evidence is any written or recorded material presented to support a party's argument or claim.

In a courtroom, documentary evidence is used to establish facts and provide proof to support a case. It is often considered more reliable than oral testimony because it provides a tangible, often unchangeable record of events, actions, or statements. However, for documentary evidence to be admissible in court, it must be relevant, authentic, and reliable.

Relevance refers to the document's direct relation to the case at hand. Authenticity means that the document is what it purports to be, not a forgery or falsification. Reliability refers to the document's trustworthiness as a source of evidence. It should be free from alterations or tampering.

The process of introducing documentary evidence in court involves several steps. First, the party intending to use the document must provide a copy to the opposing party before the trial. This is known as "discovery." During the trial, the document is formally introduced through a witness who can attest to its authenticity. The opposing party then has the opportunity to cross-examine the witness about the document. Finally, the judge or jury considers the document as part of the evidence in deciding the case.

Now, let's consider how documentary evidence could be used to prove the existence of Sasquatch, a creature of North American folklore often referred to as Bigfoot. Researchers seeking to prove Sasquatch's existence could use various forms of documentary evidence, including videos, audio recordings, photographs, and eyewitness drawings.

Photographs and video recordings of alleged Sasquatch sightings could serve as powerful documentary evidence, provided they are clear, authentic, and reliable. However, they must be carefully scrutinized for potential tampering or misinterpretation. For instance, what appears to be a Sasquatch in a blurry photo could be a bear or a human in a costume.

Footprint casts and hair samples could also serve as documentary evidence. If these physical traces match descriptions of Sasquatch but not any known animal, they could support the claim of Sasquatch's existence. However, they would likely need to be accompanied by expert testimony explaining their significance and ruling out other explanations.

Eyewitness accounts, while not documentary evidence in the traditional sense, could be recorded in written or audiovisual form and used as such. These accounts could provide detailed descriptions of Sasquatch sightings, including the creature's appearance, behavior, and location. However, like all documentary evidence, these accounts would need to be evaluated for their credibility and reliability.

Documentary evidence plays a crucial role in both legal proceedings and scientific research. Whether it's used to prove a claim in court or the existence of a legendary creature, the principles remain the same: the evidence must be relevant, authentic, and reliable.

Demonstrative Evidence: Its Role in Sasquatch Research

Demonstrative evidence, or illustrative evidence, is a type of evidence that visually represents or demonstrates a fact or concept. It is used in courtrooms to help judges, juries, and attorneys better understand the facts of a case. Demonstrative evidence can take many forms, including diagrams, charts, models, animations, simulations, and physical objects related to the case.

In a courtroom, demonstrative evidence is used to illustrate or clarify testimony and other forms of evidence. For example, a diagram of a crime scene can help jurors visualize the location of key events, while a model of a vehicle can demonstrate how an accident occurred. Demonstrative evidence can also be used to summarize complex data or information in a more understandable way, such as a chart showing a timeline of events or a graph illustrating financial losses.

However, for demonstrative evidence to be admissible in court, it must be relevant, accurate, and fair. Relevance means that the evidence must directly relate to the facts of the case. Accuracy means that the evidence must correctly represent the facts or concepts it is intended to illustrate. Fairness means that the evidence must not be misleading or prejudicial.

But how could demonstrative evidence be used to prove the existence of Sasquatch? Researchers seeking to prove Sasquatch's existence could use various forms of demonstrative evidence, including maps, models, and diagrams.

Maps of alleged Sasquatch sightings could serve as demonstrative evidence, showing the geographic distribution and frequency of sightings. These maps could help researchers identify patterns and correlations, such as a relationship between sightings and certain types of terrain or vegetation.

Models of Sasquatch, based on eyewitness descriptions and physical evidence like footprint casts, could also serve as demonstrative evidence. These models could help researchers and others visualize what Sasquatch might look like and how it might move.

Diagrams illustrating the size and shape of alleged Sasquatch footprints compared to those of known animals could serve as demonstrative evidence. These diagrams could help researchers determine whether the footprints are unique or could be attributed to another animal.

Whether demonstrative evidence is used to illustrate a point in court or the existence of a legendary creature like Sasquatch, the principles as with all other types remain the same: the evidence must be relevant, accurate, and fair.

Testimonial Evidence: Its Role in Sasquatch Research

Testimonial evidence is a type of evidence that is given orally by a witness under oath in a court of law. It is one of the most common forms of evidence and can be used to establish facts, provide context, and support or refute other evidence. Testimonial evidence can come from a variety of sources, including eyewitnesses, expert witnesses, and character witnesses.

In a courtroom, testimonial evidence is used to provide firsthand accounts of events, actions, or conditions. Eyewitnesses can describe what they saw, heard, or experienced, while expert witnesses can provide specialized knowledge or opinions based on their expertise. Character witnesses can testify about a person's character or reputation, which can be relevant in certain cases.

As with real evidence, documentary evidence, and demonstrative evidence, for testimonial evidence to be admissible in court, it must be relevant, competent, and reliable. Relevance means that the testimony must directly relate to the facts of the case. Competence refers to the witness's ability to accurately perceive, recall, and communicate their experiences. Reliability refers to the trustworthiness of the witness and their testimony.

Researchers seeking to prove Sasquatch's existence could use various forms of testimonial evidence, including eyewitness accounts and expert testimony.

Eyewitness accounts of alleged Sasquatch sightings could serve as powerful testimonial evidence. These accounts could provide detailed descriptions of Sasquatch sightings, including the creature's appearance, behavior, and location. However, like all testimonial evidence, these accounts would need to be evaluated for their credibility and reliability.

Expert testimony could also serve as testimonial evidence. For instance, a biologist could testify about the plausibility of Sasquatch's existence based on known species and ecosystems, while a forensic analyst could testify about the authenticity and significance of physical evidence like footprint casts or hair samples.

Digital Evidence: Its Role in Sasquatch Research

Digital evidence, also known as electronic evidence, is a type of evidence that is stored or transmitted in digital form. It has become increasingly important in the legal system and scientific research due to the widespread use of digital devices and the internet. Digital evidence can take many forms, including emails, text messages, social media posts, digital photos, videos, and data from GPS devices or other electronic sensors.

In a courtroom, digital evidence is used to establish facts and provide proof to support a case. For example, emails or text messages can reveal communications between parties, while digital photos or videos can provide visual evidence of events or conditions. GPS data can show a person's or vehicle's location at a specific time, while data from electronic sensors can record a wide range of physical conditions, from temperature and humidity to motion and sound.

However, for digital evidence to be admissible in court, it must be relevant, authentic, and reliable. Relevance means that the evidence must directly relate to the facts of the case. Authenticity means that the evidence must be what it purports to be, not a forgery or falsification. Reliability refers to the trustworthiness of the evidence. It should be free from alterations or tampering, and the devices or systems that produced it should be shown to be functioning correctly.

Digital photos and videos of alleged Sasquatch sightings could serve as powerful digital evidence, provided they are clear, authentic, and reliable.

Data from electronic sensors could also serve as digital evidence. For example, motion sensors or trail cameras could capture evidence of Sasquatch's presence, while audio recorders could capture sounds attributed to Sasquatch. GPS data could show the location of sightings or track the movement of Sasquatch if it were tagged with a GPS device.

As we dig deeper into the various forms of evidence utilized in our legal system on a daily basis, it becomes increasingly feasible to apply them to the realm of Sasquatch research. It becomes evident to me that although not entirely conclusive, there is a substantial amount of evidence that could be considered proof of Sasquatch's existence. The sheer number of anecdotal accounts, shared by countless eyewitnesses, presents a compelling argument worthy of trial.

When we include photographs, videos, audio recordings, expert testimonies, footprints, and even DNA samples, I firmly believe that we find an ample amount of evidence to convict the elusive Sasquatch of its existence.

13

BIGFOOT HIGH STRANGENESS: THE "WOO FACTOR" IN SASQUATCH RESEARCH: UFO ENCOUNTERS, HABITUATION, AND SCIENTIFIC SKEPTICISM

The field of Sasquatch, or Bigfoot as it is popularly known, research is riddled with a high degree of strangeness, often referred to as "woo." This term is used to describe the unexplained, paranormal, or supernatural elements that often accompany Sasquatch sightings and encounters. These elements range from UFO sightings to telepathic communication, and they have been a significant factor in keeping mainstream scientists from taking Sasquatch research seriously.

The connection between Sasquatch and UFOs is another aspect of the "woo" that has been reported by numerous witnesses. For instance, in 1973, Pennsylvania witnessed a surge in both Sasquatch and UFO sightings. In one case, a man reported seeing a Sasquatch with a glowing green orb. Moments later, a UFO was spotted in the same area. Similar reports have come from other parts of the country, linking Sasquatch sightings with strange lights or objects in the sky.

The "Bigfoot-UFO" theory was popularized by researchers like Stan Gordon, who suggested that Sasquatch might be an extraterrestrial being. This theory, while fascinating to some, further alienates mainstream scientists from Sasquatch research.

The "woo" in Sasquatch research is not limited to UFOs and psychic Sasquatches. Some researchers, like Dr. Matthew Johnson, claim that Sasquatches can cloak themselves, becoming invisible at will. Here is a summary of Dr. Johnson's alleged Sasquatch encounter that occurred on July 1, 2000.

Where do I start? Rochelle and I decided to take our children on a trip to the Oregon Caves National Park, located in the southern part of Oregon. We enjoyed a picnic lunch before embarking on a tour of the breathtaking caves. If you've never seen them, I highly recommend them.

After exiting the cave, most visitors typically turn right to head back to the gift shop and lodge. However, being recent transplants from Alaska with a love for outdoor adventures, we chose to turn left and hike up to the Big Tree, a Douglas fir with a 40-foot circumference that's estimated to be between 800 and 1,000 years old. We trekked about 2 miles into the forest, and up the mountain. During our hike, we encountered a potent smell, similar to a skunk but distinctly different.

As we continued our ascent, the trail began to curve to the right. Amidst the towering trees and thick brush, I heard a faint, rhythmic sound. Initially, I dismissed it as the pounding of my own blood vessels, a result of the strenuous hike. But as the sound grew louder, I realized it was coming from outside, not within. We all paused, confirming that we all heard the same sound.

Despite the strange sound, we pressed on, the noise growing louder and more frequent. Suddenly, my instincts kicked in. I halted my family on the trail and ventured up the hill to relieve myself, a common reaction to the "fight or flight" response. As I did so, I scanned the surrounding woods and saw something that took my breath away.

I've encountered grizzly and black bears during my hikes in Alaska, even being chased by a grizzly once. But what I saw was neither of these. It was a creature walking upright, taller than any bear, resembling a human. It was Bigfoot, or Sasquatch.

Without alarming my family, I hurried them up the mountain, keeping a vigilant eye on our surroundings. When we reached a safe spot, I confided in Rochelle about what I saw. She believed me instantly, having heard the strange sounds and smelled the unusual scent. We agreed not to tell the children to avoid causing panic.

We made it out of the woods about one and a half hours later, and while the kids browsed the gift shop, Rochelle and I debated whether to report our encounter. Ultimately, I decided to share our experience, knowing it was real and that I was sane. I reported the sighting to NPS Ranger Beverly, who believed my account.

Rochelle and I are open to discussing our experience. We believe it's important to share such encounters with the world. This is a true story that occurred on July 1, 2000, just after 5:00 pm.

In addition to his theories on Sasquatch's ability to cloak and open portals, Dr. Johnson also believes that these creatures can and are being habituated. He has made claims that he has interacted with these creatures on at least two sites in the past, one of which is where the Sasquatch is able to open portals.

Habituation and its Implications in Sasquatch Research

Habituation, in the realm of ethology and psychology, refers to the process by which an organism reduces or ceases its response to a recurring stimulus over time. This reduction in response is not due to sensory adaptation or fatigue but is a result of the organism learning that the stimulus is of no significant consequence. Essentially, habituation is a form of non-associative learning where an organism, over time, becomes accustomed to a stimulus and gradually decreases its response.

In the context of Sasquatch research, habituation refers to the process by which these otherwise elusive creatures may become accustomed to the presence of humans or human-related activities in their environment. This process is often claimed to occur in areas where Sasquatch and human territories overlap, leading to repeated encounters between the two species.

One of the most well-known examples of claimed Sasquatch habituation is the case of the "Bigfoot Field Researchers Organization" (BFRO). They have reported several instances where Sasquatches have been observed repeatedly in the same areas, suggesting a level of comfort or habituation with human presence. Another example is the "Skookum Meadow Incident" in Washington State, where researchers claimed to have found evidence of a Sasquatch repeatedly visiting a specific site, indicating possible habituation.

Janice Carter: 50 Years with Bigfoot Saga

The Janice Carter: 50 Years with Bigfoot saga is a fascinating tale that has intrigued and baffled Sasquatch enthusiasts for decades. Janice Carter, a resident of Tennessee, claims that her family has been interacting with a group of Sasquatches living on their property for over 50 years. Her story, filled with extraordinary details and claims, has been the subject of much debate and skepticism within the Bigfoot research community.

Janice's story begins in 1959 when her grandfather, James Carter, allegedly encountered a wounded Sasquatch on their property. According to Janice, James nursed the creature back to health, and in gratitude, the Sasquatch, whom they named "Fox," introduced the Carter family to his clan. This marked the beginning of a unique relationship between the Carters and the Sasquatches.

Over the years, Janice claims that her family has had numerous interactions with these creatures. She describes them as intelligent beings capable of communication, both verbally and non-verbally. Janice asserts that the Sasquatches have their own language, which she has learned to understand and speak to some extent. She also claims that they have a complex social structure, with Fox serving as the leader of the clan.

Janice's accounts of her family's interactions with the Sasquatches are filled with remarkable details. She describes them as being around 8 feet tall, with a muscular build, covered in hair, and possessing an intense, distinctive smell. According to her, they are omnivorous, consuming both plants and meat and have a particular fondness for sweets, especially cookies and candies.

One of the most controversial aspects of Janice's story is her claim that the Sasquatches have the ability to cloak themselves, becoming invisible at will. She asserts that this ability, along with their nocturnal habits and elusive nature, is why they have managed to avoid detection for so long.

Janice also claims that the Sasquatches have a deep respect for nature and live in harmony with their environment. She describes them as peaceful creatures who have never posed a threat to her family. However, she also notes that they are fiercely protective of their territory and will defend it if they feel threatened.

In 2002, Janice co-authored a book with Mary Green titled *50 Years with Bigfoot: Tennessee Chronicles of Co-Existence*, where she detailed her family's experiences with the Sasquatches. The book, filled with anecdotes and personal accounts, has been met with mixed reactions. While some find her story compelling and believe in its authenticity, others dismiss it as a hoax or the product of an overactive imagination.

Despite the skepticism and controversy surrounding her story, Janice remains steadfast in her claims. She continues to share her experiences and advocate for the recognition and protection of Sasquatches. Whether one believes in her story or not, the Janice

Carter: 50 Years with Bigfoot saga remains a fascinating chapter in the history of Sasquatch lore.

If they do exist, the habituation of a creature like Sasquatch could be immensely helpful in understanding and studying them. If Sasquatches become accustomed to human presence, they may be less likely to flee or hide, allowing researchers to observe their behavior more closely. This could provide valuable insights into their social structure, diet, mating habits, and other aspects of their ecology and behavior. Habituation could also potentially facilitate more direct interactions with Sasquatches, such as baiting or luring them to specific locations for observation or data collection.

However, habituation also carries significant risks and potential negative impacts for Sasquatches. Increased comfort with human presence could lead Sasquatches to venture closer to human settlements, increasing the risk of conflict. They could become targets for poaching or harassment, or they could be hit by vehicles if they start crossing roads more frequently. Habituation could also lead to changes in Sasquatch behavior that are detrimental to their survival, such as increased reliance on human food sources or decreased wariness of other potential threats.

Additionally, habituation could have negative impacts on Sasquatch populations at a broader scale. If Sasquatches become more visible and less elusive, this could increase public interest and pressure for their habitat, potentially leading to habitat destruction or disturbance. This could also fuel commercial exploitation, such as Sasquatch-themed tourism or entertainment, which could further disrupt their habitats and lifestyles.

If Sasquatches do exist, habituation could potentially provide valuable opportunities for studying them, it also carries significant risks and potential negative impacts. Therefore, any attempts to habituate Sasquatches should be approached with caution, and measures should be taken to minimize potential harm. This includes maintaining a respectful distance, minimizing disturbance, and prioritizing the welfare and conservation of Sasquatches above scientific curiosity or commercial interests.

Others believe in inter-dimensional Sasquatches, suggesting that these creatures can move between different dimensions, which explains their elusive nature. While these hypotheses and stories add a layer of intrigue to Sasquatch research, they also contribute to the skepticism and dismissal by the scientific community. Mainstream scientists demand empirical evidence, which is often lacking in these high-strangeness cases. The "woo" factor, while appealing to some, tends to undermine the credibility of Sasquatch research in the eyes of many scientists.

Former Air Force intelligence officer and *Alien Digest* publisher, Ron Rummel, tragically passed away on August 6, 1993, purportedly from a self-inflicted gunshot wound to the mouth.

The *Digest*, under Rummel's stewardship, produced seven exclusive issues, which are now extremely difficult to find. One undeniable fact is that Rummel's publication was delving into controversial topics, including the possibility of an Alien/Bigfoot connection. In one issue, Rummel wrote about an incident that occurred in 1977. He describes a hypnosis session where a young man described the following to the hypnotist.

> I see Bigfoot creatures coming out of a cave, the cave has a redness to it down the tunnel. There is a saucer on four legs sitting on the ground next to a tree, the only tree around. The Bigfoot creatures are coming out of the cave with large metal boxes and large round canisters. They're stacking these boxes and canisters next to the tree. Men are now coming down steps from the saucers. The Bigfoot creatures start to move around. These are not men at all, they're small bigheaded beings.
>
> These Bigheads are telling the creatures to open one of the canisters for some kind of inspection. One Bigfoot creature is opening the top of one of the canisters. It's a dark red blood- like liquid with purple

specks of slime, there are what also what appear to be tiny specks of bones. The three Bigfoot creatures and the small Bigheads are turned away from the smell.

The aliens were afraid of some kind of mix-up and did not want to carry toxic, deadly compounds. They seem to be thinking that this is human waste of some sort and glad it's not something else. The faces on these aliens are very unfriendly and mean looking. They tell the Bigfoot creatures to load the metal boxes and canisters on the flying saucer. Pause....We're taking off now.

'Are you traveling on the flying saucer?' [asked the hypnotist]

'Yes I am.'

'Please go on.' [said the hypnotist]

These aliens seem unable to see me, they are always walking by me. The ship has a crew of three, we are already in space, and it has just been seconds. I can see a big window where these aliens are looking out of. They're in chairs that mold to their bodies. We're heading toward the Moon, to stop there. [pause]

We're here and it seemed like no time at all. One alien has been told to drop the containers; I'm going to follow him. We're about 50 feet from the surface of the Moon and he's pouring over this liquid from the boxes, and he does not like it at all. He's thinking they're going to need a different dumping zone. He is also thinking that we have this to look forward to as a fitting end.

I now seemed to be going outside the craft. [long Pause]

I see a very large ship here where I'm at now. It's sitting between two mountains in a valley. It's large with rocks all over it just hovering there. I want to say it's a mile long, but I know it's shorter than this. [pause]

I am in now. The ship is huge on the inside, with no levels of one side which makes it look huge. I'm on the first level by a door, there in a cage is a Bigfoot creature who knows he is trapped, he is trying to bend the bars of the cage. I'm closer to him now...He is very mad.... he seems to be very frightened at something that is going to happen to him.

The large door that is next to me just opened and inside is a smaller door that is opening. There's a Bigfoot creature locked into a big chair and these bigheaded aliens have electronic devices all over him, and he's mad but he can't do anything about it. One alien is telling the other one to shut the door before the other one sees what is going on, and who opened the door in the first place?

I now seem to be drifting to the top of this craft. I'm now on the top deck of this ship where I can see everything. This thing is huge, you could fit a battleship in here! There is a Bighead up here with his back turned on me. I'm up real close to him now; he can feel something is wrong. He looks at me. Hell, he can see me! He's staring at me to be sure he sees me. He's reaching for a metal object on the wall; he pressed it down....'

"At that time the young man woke up without being taken out of his deep sleep. He was very calm and said that at the last second on the Mothership, he knew that the Bighead could see him. Take this as you may."

Despite the high strangeness, there are researchers who approach the subject from a more scientific perspective, focusing on physical evidence like footprints, hair samples, and video footage. However, the "woo" often overshadows these efforts, keeping Sasquatch firmly in the realm of the unexplained.

The "woo" in Sasquatch research is a double-edged sword. On the one hand, it adds a layer of mystery and intrigue that attracts many to the field. On the other hand, it serves as a barrier, preventing mainstream scientific acceptance of Sasquatch as a legitimate area of study.

I firmly hold the view that regardless of how outlandish they may seem, personal accounts from those who claim to have encountered Sasquatch have a role to play in its research. In the pursuit of rigorous research, it's crucial to take into account all available data, even if it contradicts your initial hypothesis. However, I'm not implying that every single account should be accepted without question. I believe that until we can distinguish between the "woo" or unproven claims and the empirical or evidence-based facts, Sasquatch research may continue to face challenges in gaining scientific acceptance.

Extraordinary evidence is a concept derived from the phrase "extraordinary claims require extraordinary evidence" (ECREE), which was popularized by Carl Sagan, a renowned astrophysicist and science communicator. This principle is a pillar of the scientific method, which emphasizes skepticism until substantial evidence is presented. It essentially means that the more a claim deviates from the norm or challenges established understanding, the stronger the evidence is needed to support it.

In the context of claims about the habituation of Sasquatch, or Bigfoot, or their connection to UFOs, aliens, or inter-dimensional beings, this principle is particularly relevant. These claims are considered extraordinary because they challenge established scientific understanding in fields such as biology, physics, and anthropology. For instance, the existence of Sasquatch, a large, hairy bipedal creature, is not recognized by mainstream science due to a lack of physical evidence such as bones, hair, or feces that can be analyzed using standard scientific methods.

Similarly, claims that Sasquatch is connected to UFOs, aliens, or is an inter-dimensional being are also extraordinary. They challenge our understanding of physics, astronomy, and biology. For example, the idea of inter-dimensional travel implies the existence of dimensions beyond the three spatial, and one temporal, dimensions we experience, a concept not currently supported by empirical evidence.

Therefore, individuals making these claims would need to provide extraordinary evidence to support them. This could include clear, high-resolution photographic or video evidence, physical evidence that can be analyzed in a lab (like hair or fecal samples that contain DNA not matching any known species), or reliable eyewitness accounts corroborated by additional evidence.

In the case of connections to UFOs or aliens, evidence might include materials of extraterrestrial origin, or detailed, consistent accounts of encounters that match our understanding of physics and biology. For inter-dimensional claims, evidence could include a demonstration of inter-dimensional travel or phenomena that cannot be explained by our current understanding of physics.

It's important to note that anecdotal evidence, personal testimonies, or blurry images are typically not considered extraordinary evidence because they are prone to human error, misinterpretation, or even deliberate deception. Extraordinary evidence must be objective, verifiable, and stand up to rigorous scrutiny by the scientific community.

While the habituation of Sasquatch, or their connection to UFOs, aliens, or inter-dimensional beings, is fascinating, these extraordinary claims require extraordinary evidence. Until such evidence is provided and withstands scientific scrutiny, skepticism remains the appropriate response.

14

THE FASCINATION WITH MONSTERS: CRYPTIDS, ESCAPISM, AND THE MODERN WORLD

The human fascination with monsters, particularly cryptids like Sasquatch, is a complex and intriguing phenomenon. I want to dig a little deeper into this fascination, exploring the psychological, sociological, and cultural factors that contribute to our collective obsession with these elusive creatures.

Cryptids, by definition, are creatures whose existence is suggested but not confirmed by scientific consensus. Sasquatch, the Loch Ness Monster, and the Chupacabra are arguably the big three. These creatures, despite their lack of empirical evidence, have captured the human imagination for centuries, if not millennia.

The fascination with cryptids can be traced back to our primal instincts. As a species, humans have always been storytellers. We have used stories to make sense of the world around us, to teach lessons, and to entertain. Cryptids, with their mysterious nature and elusive existence, provide the perfect fodder for our storytelling instincts. They represent the unknown, the unexplored, and the unexplained -- elements that are inherently fascinating to us.

Cryptids also tap into our innate fear and curiosity of the unknown. They represent the wild, the untamed, and the dangerous -- aspects of nature that we have largely tamed or eliminated in our modern, urbanized world. In this sense, cryptids serve as a reminder of our primal past, a past where we were not the dominant species and where danger lurked in every shadow.

This ties in with the concept of escapism. In our fast-paced, highly structured modern world, many of us yearn for a break from the mundane. We crave adventure, excitement, and mystery -- elements that are often lacking in our daily lives. Cryptids, with their elusive nature and the mystery surrounding their existence, provide an escape from the ordinary. They allow us to imagine a world that is not fully understood, a world where adventure and danger are just around the corner.

The search for cryptids also provides a sense of purpose and community. For many, the hunt for these elusive creatures is more than just a hobby -- it's a mission, a quest for truth. This quest brings people together, creating a community of like-minded individuals who share a common goal. In a world where traditional communities are increasingly fragmented, this sense of belonging and purpose can be incredibly appealing.

Our interest in cryptids also reflects our desire for discovery and exploration. Despite the advances in science and technology, there is still so much we don't know about our world. The existence of cryptids represents one of these unknowns, a mystery waiting to be solved. The pursuit of these creatures, therefore, is a manifestation of our innate desire to explore and discover.

In our fast-paced modern world, these creatures provide a much-needed escape from the ordinary, a reminder of our primal past, and a mystery to be solved. As long as these elements remain appealing, the obsession with cryptids is likely to endure.

Escapism: The Sasquatch Phenomenon and Modern-Day Diversions

Escapism, as a concept, refers to the human tendency to seek distraction and relief from unpleasant or mundane realities, often by immersing oneself in imaginative activities or entertainment. This chapter will explore the role of escapism in the human belief in cryptids like Sasquatch and compare it with other forms of modern-day escapism such as sports and social media platforms like Instagram, TikTok, Facebook, and YouTube.

The belief in Sasquatch, or Bigfoot, is a form of escapism that taps into our primal instincts and our love for mystery and adventure. Despite the lack of empirical evidence, many people are drawn to the idea of a large, hairy bipedal creature roaming the wilderness. This belief allows them to escape from their everyday lives and immerse themselves in a world of mystery and exploration. It provides a sense of excitement and wonder that is often lacking in our modern, structured world.

In many ways, the belief in Sasquatch is similar to the obsession with sports. Both provide a form of escapism that allows people to immerse themselves in a world that is separate from their everyday lives. Sports, like the search for Sasquatch, provide a sense of excitement, community, and purpose. They allow people to escape from their mundane realities and immerse themselves in a world of competition, camaraderie, and achievement.

Social media platforms like Instagram, TikTok, Facebook, and YouTube offer another form of escapism. These platforms allow users to curate and present an idealized version of their lives, to connect with others, and to immerse themselves in a world of entertainment and information. Like the belief in Sasquatch and the obsession with sports, social media provides a form of escapism that allows users to escape from their everyday realities.

However, while the belief in Sasquatch and the obsession with sports are generally positive forms of escapism, social media can have both positive and negative effects. On the positive side, social media can provide a sense of community, a platform for self-expression, and a source of entertainment and information. On the negative side, it can lead to feelings of inadequacy, isolation, and addiction. The curated and idealized images presented on social media can create unrealistic expectations and pressure to live up to an unattainable standard.

In comparison, the belief in Sasquatch, while it may be seen as irrational by some, is a form of escapism that is largely harmless. It provides a sense of wonder and excitement, a connection to nature, and a community of like-minded individuals. It allows believers to escape from their everyday lives and immerse themselves in a world of mystery and exploration.

Escapism, whether in the form of belief in Sasquatch, obsession with sports, or use of social media, plays a significant role in our lives. It provides a means of distraction and relief from our everyday realities and a way to connect with others and express ourselves. However, like any other human behavior, it can have both positive and negative effects. It is therefore important to approach escapism with a sense of balance and mindfulness, to ensure that it serves as a source of enjoyment and enrichment, rather than a source of stress or dissatisfaction.

15

THE TRUTH BEHIND THE LEGEND: IS SASQUATCH REAL OR A PRODUCT OF OUR IMAGINATION

After analyzing hundreds of first-hand accounts, I've found that most witnesses can be grouped into several categories. The first group most likely saw or experienced exactly what they claimed. Some saw or experienced something that likely only occurred in their imagination. A few witnesses' sightings or sounds that they attributed to Sasquatch, are more probable misidentifications of a known creature. The final group of witnesses have no genuine experiences and fabricate their tales for various reasons.

Personal stories comprise the bulk of evidence for Sasquatch's existence, but due to the intricacies of human nature, they are the hardest to verify. Despite my skepticism, considering the vast number of claims, I do believe it's highly probable that many have had a genuine encounter with a Sasquatch.

Most skeptics will tell you; the truth is that they do not exist. Over the years I have heard many explanations for the thousands of anecdotal accounts shared by those that claim to have seen one of these creatures. Some have suggested that the Sasquatch phenomenon is all a product of mass hallucination or mass hysteria.

Mass hallucination, also known as collective hallucination, is a psychological phenomenon where a group of people, simultaneously and collectively, perceive a sensation or image that is not present in reality. This phenomenon is often associated with high-stress situations, shared beliefs, or cultural expectations. It is a complex and intriguing subject that has been studied extensively in the fields of psychology, sociology, and neuroscience.

Hallucinations are typically associated with individual experiences, often linked to conditions such as schizophrenia, drug use, or neurological disorders. However, mass hallucinations are unique in that they involve a group of people sharing the same hallucinatory experience. This phenomenon is relatively rare and often occurs in situations where the group is under extreme stress or fear, or where there is a strong expectation or belief in a particular event or entity.

One of the most famous examples of mass hallucination occurred during the Salem Witch Trials in the late 17th century. The young girls who accused others of witchcraft reported seeing and experiencing things that were not there, and their hallucinations were shared by others in their community, leading to mass hysteria and the execution of twenty people.

Another well-documented example is the Spring Heeled Jack sightings that occurred in the 19th century. The phenomenon of Spring Heeled Jack, a character from English folklore, began in the Victorian era, with the first sightings reported in 1837. The entity was described as a devil-like figure with a terrifying appearance, capable of making extraordinary leaps, hence the name 'Spring Heeled Jack'. The sightings were primarily concentrated in Greater London, the Midlands, and later Scotland.

The first recorded encounter with Spring Heeled Jack was in October 1837, when a servant girl named Mary Stevens was walking to Lavender Hill, London. She reported being attacked by a mysterious figure who leaped at her from a dark alley. The figure, she claimed, had a terrifying and devilish appearance, with clawed hands and eyes that resembled red balls of fire. The next day, the same figure reportedly attacked a carriage, causing the driver to lose control and crash.

The most famous encounter occurred in February 1838, when a young woman named Jane Alsop reported that a man had come to her father's house in East London, claiming to be a police officer and asking for a light, saying he had caught Spring Heeled Jack in the lane. When she brought the man a candle, she noticed that he wore a large cloak and had glowing eyes. Suddenly, he threw off the cloak, revealing a terrifying figure with a devil-like appearance. He then attacked her with his claws, attempting to tear her gown.

The sightings continued throughout the 19th century, with reports of encounters in the Midlands and even as far north as Scotland. The last reported sighting of Spring Heeled Jack was in Liverpool in 1904.

The descriptions of Spring Heeled Jack varied, but most accounts described him as having a terrifying appearance, with fiery eyes, a pointed chin, large ears, and a nose that was sharp and bird-like. He was often reported to be wearing a helmet and a tight-fitting white oilskin suit. Most notably, he was said to be capable of making extraordinary leaps.

Theories about the true nature of Spring Heeled Jack are numerous. Some suggest that he was an extraterrestrial being, while others believe he was a demon or the devil himself. Another theory posits that he was a human prankster using springs to achieve his extraordinary leaps.

One popular theory suggests that the sightings were a form of mass hysteria, fueled by the fears and superstitions of the Victorian era. This theory is supported by the fact that many of the sightings occurred in periods of social unrest, such as the Chartist movement in the 1840s.

Another theory suggests that the sightings were a form of moral panic, a reaction to the rapid social changes of the Victorian era. This theory posits that Spring Heeled Jack was a symbolic representation of the fears and anxieties of the time, a figure who embodied the dangers of the city and the threat of the unknown.

Despite the numerous theories, the true nature of Spring Heeled Jack remains a mystery. The sightings have become a part of English folklore, a chilling reminder of the fears and superstitions of the Victorian era.

In the context of Sasquatch encounters, some skeptics argue that much like the Salem Witch Trials or the Spring Heeled Jack sightings, mass hallucination could explain the numerous sightings reported across North America. The hypothesis suggests that the cultural expectation and widespread belief in the existence of this creature could lead groups of people to collectively hallucinate its presence.

As we have already discussed, Sasquatch is deeply ingrained in North American folklore, with countless stories, films, and television shows dedicated to the creature. This cultural saturation could create a strong expectation or belief in Sasquatch, particularly in areas where sightings are commonly reported. When a group of people venture into these areas, particularly if they are under stress or fear, they may be more susceptible to a collective hallucination of Sasquatch.

But it's important to note that mass hallucination is a controversial explanation for Sasquatch encounters. Critics argue that it is unlikely that different groups of people, in different locations and times, could all hallucinate the same creature with similar characteristics. Furthermore, physical evidence such as footprints and hair samples, which cannot be explained by hallucination, have been found in association with some Sasquatch sightings.

While mass hallucination provides a potential explanation for some Sasquatch encounters, it is not universally accepted. The phenomenon of mass hallucination itself is complex and not fully understood, and its application to Sasquatch encounters is a topic of ongoing debate. As with many aspects of psychology and folklore, the truth may be a complex interplay of belief, perception, and reality.

Does this mean that Sasquatch is simply something that was created in the minds of those that choose to believe? I say not so fast. Given the abundance of physical evidence, including video footage, footprints, anecdotal accounts, and photographs, it is essential to compare this evidence with the potential argument that it is all fabricated or merely a mass hallucination. However, after careful analysis and consideration of the facts, it becomes evident that Sasquatch may indeed exist.

As we have already discussed, numerous videos have surfaced over the years, capturing what appears to be a large, bipedal creature resembling the description of Sasquatch. These videos often depict the creature in its natural habitat, displaying distinct characteristics such as its towering height, broad shoulders, and a peculiar gait. While skeptics argue that these videos could be hoaxes, it is crucial to note that many of them have undergone rigorous analysis by experts in the field, who have concluded that they are genuine and unaltered.

Secondly, footprints attributed to Sasquatch have been discovered in various locations around the world. These footprints exhibit remarkable similarities, characterized by their immense size, unique dermal ridges, and a distinct mid-tarsal break. Skeptics may argue that these footprints could be the result of elaborate pranks or misidentifications of other animal tracks. However, the consistency in size and morphology across different regions and time periods suggests a common source, supporting the existence of a large, unidentified primate species.

Anecdotal accounts also contribute to the body of evidence supporting the existence of Sasquatch. Witnesses from diverse backgrounds and locations have reported encounters with this elusive creature. These accounts often share common details, describing a towering, hairy creature with human-like features. While individual testimonies can be subject to skepticism, the sheer number of consistent reports from credible witnesses cannot be easily dismissed.

These accounts span decades and come from individuals with no apparent motive to fabricate such encounters.

Furthermore, photographs of Sasquatch have been captured, some of which have undergone extensive analysis by experts. While some photographs may be blurry or inconclusive, there are instances where clear and detailed images have been obtained. These photographs provide additional visual evidence of a large, bipedal creature that aligns with the descriptions provided by eyewitnesses and other forms of evidence.

When considering the vast amount of physical evidence, including video footage, footprints, anecdotal accounts, and photographs, it becomes increasingly difficult to dismiss the existence of Sasquatch as a fabrication or mass hallucination. The consistency and convergence of these different forms of evidence, along with the analysis conducted by experts in relevant fields, strongly support the notion that an unidentified primate species may indeed exist.

While further research and investigation are necessary to definitively prove its existence, the available evidence provides a compelling case for the reality of this elusive creature. Ultimately, the truth behind the legend lies with each of you and what you choose to believe.

BONUS VIDEO SECTION

Scan QR code for bonus content.

REFERENCES
SELECTED SOURCES & BIBLIOGRAPHY

Byrne, P. (1976). The Search for Bigfoot: Monster, Myth, or Man. Pocket Books.

Gloss, M. (2000). Wild Life. Houghton Mifflin.

Pyle, R. M. (1995). Where Bigfoot Walks: Crossing the Dark Divide. Houghton Mifflin.

Wallace, D. R. (2003). The Klamath Knot: Explorations of Myth and Evolution. (2nd ed.). University of California Press.

Washington National Guard. (2023). Washington National Guard Website. https://mil.wa.gov/the-legend-of-bigfoot

Walls, R. E. (1996). Bigfoot. In J. H. Brunvand (Ed.), American Folklore: An Encyclopedia. Garland Publishing, Inc.

Freeman, M. (2022). Freeman Bigfoot Files. Hangar 1 Publishing. https://books.google.com/books?id=y7CgEAAAQBAJ

Nickell, J. (2017). Bigfoot As Big Myth: 7 Phases of Mythmaking. Skeptical Inquirer. https://web.archive.org/web/20180826145056/https://www.csi-cop.org/si/show/bigfoot_as_big_myth_seven_phases_of_mythmaking

Bigfoot Field Research Organization. (n.d.). Geographical Database of Sasquatch Sightings and Reports. https://www.bfro.net

Associated Press. (n.d.). DNA tests to help crack mystery of Bigfoot or Yeti existence. The Australian. http://www.theaustralian.com.au/news/world/dna-to-test-bigfoot-mystery/story-e6frg6so-1226365397311

Radford, B. (2012, November 6). Bigfoot: Man-Monster or Myth? Live Science. http://www.livescience.com/24598-bigfoot.html

Jilek-Aall, L. (1972). What is a Sasquatch — or the Problematics of Reality Testing. Canadian Psychiatric Association Journal. https://doi.org/10.1177%2F070674377201700312

Mancini, M. (2015, January 10). 11 Crazy Bigfoot Conspiracy Theories. The Week. https://theweek.com/articles/466777/11-crazy-bigfoot-conspiracy-theories

Kimmick, E. (2012, August 19). 'Sasquatch Watch' researcher keeps on looking for rock-throwing beast. Missoulian. https://missoulian.com/news/state-and-regional/sasquatch-watch-researcher-keeps-on-looking-for-rock-throwing-beast

Enzastiga, A. (2018, September 20). The hunt to prove the existence of Sasquatch. The Daily Iowan. https://dailyiowan.com/2018/09/20/the-hunt-to-prove-the-existence-of-sasquatch/

First Draft News. (n.d.). The psychology of misinformation: why we're vulnerable. https://firstdraftnews.org/articles/the-psychology-of-misinformation-why-were-vulnerable/

Roosevelt, T. (1903). The wilderness hunter; an account of the big game of the United States and its chase with horse, hound and rifle. Gebbie and company. https://www.loc.gov/item/03003862/

References

Alford, G. (2000, October 23). Idaho State University Researcher Coordinates Analysis of Body Imprint That May Belong to a Sasquatch. http://www.bfro.net/news/body-cast/ISU_press_rel_cast.asp

Coleman, L. (n.d.). UltimateGA Bigfoot Hoax Timeline: 2008. Cryptomundo. https://cryptomundo.com/cryptozoo-news/hoax-tl-08/

Fleagle, J., & Gilbert, C. (2011). Primate Evolution. In N. Rowe & M. Myers (Eds.), All the World's Primates. Primate Conservation, Inc. http://alltheworldsprimates.org/John_Fleagle_Public.aspx

Regal, B. (2008). Amateur versus professional: the search for Bigfoot. Endeavour. https://doi.org/10.1016%2Fj.endeavour.2008.04.005

Lopatin, A. V., Maschenko, E. N., & Dac, L. X. (2022). Gigantopithecus blacki (Primates, Ponginae) from the Lang Trang Cave (Northern Vietnam): The Latest Gigantopithecus in the Late Pleistocene? Doklady Biological Sciences. https://link.springer.com/10.1134/S0012496622010069

Srivastava, R. P. (2009). Morphology Of the Primates And Human Evolution. PHI Learning Pvt. Ltd.

Fleagle, J. G. (2013). Primate Adaptation and Evolution. Academic Press.

Cameron, D. W. (2004). Hominid Adaptations and Extinctions. UNSW Press.

Native Americans Language. (n.d.). Native Americans Language Website. http://www.native-languages.org/legends-bigfoot.htm

Perry, D. (2018, January 26). How a 1924 Bigfoot battle on Mt. St. Helens helped launch a legend. The Oregonian. https://www.oregonlive.com/history/2018/01/1924_bigfoot_battle_on_mt_st_h.html

Green, J. (1973). Bigfoot: On the Track of the Sasquatch. Ballantine Books.

Sanderson, I. T. (2008). Abominable Snowmen - Legend Come to Life. Cosimo Inc.

Harry and the Hendersons. (n.d.). [VHS]. ISBN 1558807225.

Discovering Bigfoot Documentary. (n.d.). Retrieved from https://www.imdb.com/title/tt7058016/plotsummary/?ref_=tt_ov_pl

Merriam-Webster. (n.d.). Remote. In Merriam-Webster.com dictionary. Retrieved from https://www.merriam-webster.com/dictionary/remote

Merriam-Webster. (n.d.). Ice water. In Merriam-Webster.com dictionary. Retrieved from https://www.merriam-webster.com/dictionary/ice%20water

Rowsell, G. J., Reaburn, P., Toone, R., Smith, M., & Coutts, A. J. (2014). Effect of run training and cold-water immersion on subsequent cycle training quality in high-performance triathletes. Journal of Strength and Conditioning Research, 28(6), 1664–1672. https://doi.org/10.1519/JSC.0000000000000455

Merriam-Webster. (n.d.). Pareidolia. In Merriam-Webster.com dictionary. Retrieved from https://www.merriam-webster.com/dictionary/pareidolia

Merriam-Webster. (n.d.). Scientific method. In Merriam-Webster.com dictionary. Retrieved from https://www.merriam-webster.com/dictionary/scientific%20method

Einstein, A. (2009). On the method of theoretical physics. In A. Harris (Trans.), Einstein's essays in science (pp. 12–21). Dover. (Original work published 1934)

Newton, I. (1999). Philosophiæ Naturalis Principia Mathematica [Mathematical principles of natural philosophy]. In I. B. Cohen, A. Whitman, & J. Budenz (Trans.), The

Principia: Mathematical principles of natural philosophy (pp. 371–946). University of California Press. (Original work published 1726)

Dixon, W. H. (2003). Personal history of Lord Bacon from unpublished papers. Kessinger.

American Psychiatric Association. (2013). Diagnostic and statistical manual of mental disorders (5th ed.). https://doi.org/10.1176/appi.books.9780890425596

Jones, E. A. (1995). National assessment of college student learning: Identifying college graduates' essential skills in writing, speech and listening, and critical thinking. National Center on Postsecondary Teaching, Learning, and Assessment. Retrieved from http://files.eric.ed.gov/fulltext/ED383255.pdf

Dictionary.com. (2013, June 25). Lexical investigations: Critical thinking. Retrieved from http://www.dictionary.com/e/critical-thinking/

Solomon, S. A. (2002). Two systems of reasoning. In Heuristics and biases: The psychology of intuitive judgment. Cambridge University Press.

Goodall, J. (1971). In the shadow of man. Houghton Mifflin.

Rowe, N., & Myers, M. (Eds.). (2016). All the world's primates. Pogonias Press.

Strier, K. B. (2017). Primate behavioral ecology (5th ed.). Routledge.

Seyfarth, R. M., Cheney, D. L., & Marler, P. (1980). Monkey responses to three different alarm calls: Evidence of predator classification and semantic communication. Science, 210(4471).

Stanford, C. B. (2017). Goodall, Jane. In A. Fuentes (Ed.), The international encyclopedia of primatology (Vol. A–G). John Wiley & Sons.

Zuberbühler, K., Jenny, D., & Bshary, R. (1999). The predator deterrence function of primate alarm calls. Ethology, 105(6), 477–490.

Wiens, F., & Zitzmann, A. (2003). Social structure of the solitary slow loris Nycticebus coucang (Lorisidae). Journal of Zoology, 261(1), 35–46.

Digby, L. J., Ferrari, S. F., & Saltzman, W. (2011). Callitrichines: The role of competition in cooperatively breeding species. In C. J. Campbell, A. Fuentes, K. C. MacKinnon, S. K. Bearder, & R. M. Stumpf (Eds.), Primates in perspective (2nd ed., pp. 91–102). Oxford University Press.

Smart Cities Dive. (n.d.). Effects of population growth on land use. Retrieved from https://www.smartcitiesdive.com/ex/sustainablecitiescollective/effects-population-growth-land-use/7560/

Merriam-Webster. (n.d.). Evidence. In Merriam-Webster.com dictionary. Retrieved from https://www.merriam-webster.com/dictionary/evidence

Noffke, N., Christian, D., Wacey, D., & Hazen, R. M. (2013). Microbially induced sedimentary structures recording an ancient ecosystem in the ca. 3.48-billion-year-old Dresser Formation, Pilbara, Western Australia. Astrobiology, 13(12), 1103–1124. https://doi.org/10.1089/ast.2013.1030

Bell, E. A., Boehnike, P., Harrison, T. M., et al. (2015). Potentially biogenic carbon preserved in a 4.1-billion-year-old zircon. Proc. Natl. Acad. Sci. U.S.A, 112(47), 14518–14521. https://doi.org/10.1073/pnas.1517557112

Wilson, M. A., Palmer, T. J., & Taylor, P. D. (1994). Earliest preservation of soft-bodied fossils by epibiont bioimmuration: Upper Ordovician of Kentucky. Lethaia, 27(3),

References

269–270. https://doi.org/10.1111/j.1502-3931.1994.tb01420.x

Green, M. A., & Carter, J. (n.d.). 50 years with Bigfoot: Tennessee chronicles of co-existence. Unspecified Vendor.

Sagan, C. (2011). Broca's Brain: Reflections on the romance of science. Random House Publishing Group. (Original work published 1979)

Merriam-Webster. (n.d.). Escapism. In Merriam-Webster.com dictionary. Retrieved from https://www.merriam-webster.com/dictionary/escapism

Behrensmeyer, A.K., 1978. Taphonomic and ecologic information from bone weathering. Paleobiology, 4(2), pp.150-162.

Lyman, R.L., 1994. Vertebrate taphonomy. Cambridge University Press.

Martin, L.D., 1989. Fossil history of the terrestrial Carnivora. Carnivore behavior, ecology, and evolution, 1, pp.536-568.

Meldrum, D.J., 2007. Sasquatch: Legend meets science. Forge Books.

ABOUT THE AUTHOR

Brian, a native of northwestern Georgia, has always been intrigued by the unexplained. Growing up, he heard tales of mysterious, hairy creatures in the mountains near his home. After a personal encounter as a child, he became deeply engrossed in the world of Sasquatch. Following a sixteen-year stint in law enforcement, Brian turned his passion into a hobby by starting a podcast. By 2022, this hobby had evolved into a full-time job as his *Sasquatch Odyssey* podcast became one of the most listened-to Sasquatch encounters shows on the air. He continued his quest to unravel the Sasquatch enigma through interviews with hundreds of witnesses and field research on his forty-acre property in North Carolina.

Brian has been a guest on numerous podcasts and has been featured on television shows on the *Vice Network* and *Tubi*. He is a skilled public speaker and host and has taken part in Sasquatch conferences and festivals across the United States. He is the founder and CEO of *Paranormal World Productions, LLC*. In addition to *Sasquatch Odyssey*, Brian also hosts the *True Crime Odyssey* and *That Bigfoot Podcast*.

AFTERWORD

Go to <u>hangaripublishing.com</u> to learn more about the Authors and stay up to date with their newest releases.

www.ingramcontent.com/pod-product-compliance
Lightning Source LLC
Chambersburg PA
CBHW051411050726
47595CB00010B/4014